Second Edition

Making Fun Out of Nothing at All

101 Great Games That Need No Props

Anthony Burcher and Mike Burcher

©2011 Healthy Learning. Second edition. All rights reserved. Printed in the United States.

No part of this book may be reproduced, stored in a retrieval system, or transmitted, in any form or by any means, electronic, mechanical, photocopying, recording, or otherwise, without the prior permission of Healthy Learning. Throughout this book, the masculine shall be deemed to include the feminine and vice versa.

Scripture quotations are from New Revised Standard Version Bible, copyright © 1989 National Council of the Churches of Christ in the United States of America. Used by permission. All rights reserved.

ISBN: 978-1-60679-173-8
Library of Congress Control Number: 2011927104
Cover design: Studio J Art & Design
Book layout: Studio J Art & Design
Front cover photo: Hemera/Thinkstock
Text photos: Mike Burcher

Healthy Learning
P.O. Box 1828
Monterey, CA 93942
www.healthylearning.com

Dedication

To our ARW family, who help us experience joy through art, recreation, and worship.
In Christ's name we play!

Acknowledgments

Special thanks to Joel Winchip and the 2010 Recreation Leadership in Christian Education class of Presbyterian College in Clinton, South Carolina, for their enthusiasm in playing and being photographed for this resource. Thanks to the Makemie Woods summer staff members who also posed for photographs and carry this recreation philosophy into the world. Thanks to the "Sisters 'n Friends" quilters for their general silliness and devotion to their art. And, finally, many thanks to the Annual Recreation Workshop family who taught us well, who continue to teach us, and who are missionaries for laughter in a world desperately needing to smile.

Contents

Dedication 3
Acknowledgments 4
Preface 9
Introduction 10
How to Use This Book 12

Chapter 1: Top 10 Tips for Effective Recreation Leadership 13

Chapter 2: Thou Shalt Play Safe: Avoiding the Seven Sometimes Deadly Sins of Recreation Leadership 19

Chapter 3: Mixers and Party Starters 23
    #1: 15-Second Autobiography
    #2: Amazing Adjective
    #3: Cliché Mixer Party Starter
    #4: Get to Know You Marathon
    #5: Here I Sit in the Grass
    #6: King Nebuchadnezzar
    #7: Name Zoom
    #8: Partner Mixer
    #9: Name-Dropper
    #10: Sound Effect Name Game

Chapter 4: Group Games 35
    #11: Aardvarks, Ducks, and Lambs
    #12: Cliché Shout
    #13: Echoes and Double Echoes
    #14: Fast Math
    #15: Sign Language Shoot-Out
    #16: Firecrackers
    #17: Gossip/Physical Gossip
    #18: Without Anyone Else Knowing …

#19: Human Keyboard
#20: Spy
#21: Machine Charades
#22: North and South
#23: Rain Dance
#24: Simon Says Time Warp
#25: Simon Says Swap
#26: Singing Charades
#27: Statues
#28: Thumb Grab
#29: Touch Twister
#30: Two-Team Spelling Bee

Chapter 5: Circle Games 55
#31: About-Face
#32: Anatomy Lesson
#33: Are You the Spy?
#34: Big Bunny
#35: C'mon
#36: Catch the Leader
#37: Categories
#38: Considering Cap
#39: Countdown
#40: Cross Your Palms
#41: Eye Contact
#42: Gotcha
#43: Just Like
#44: Noah's Ark
#45: One Frog
#46: Spontaneous Zoo
#47: This Is an Eagle
#48: Wanna Buy a Duck?
#49: What's Your Sign?
#50: Zip-Zap-Pop
#51: Zoom and Mooz

Chapter 6: Mind Games 83
   #52: Bang-Bang-Bang
   #53: Bugs
   #54: Cash Only Store
   #55: Costume Party
   #56: Draw the Man
   #57: Fantastic Fruits (Big Fruits/Little Fruits)
   #58: I Like Apples
   #59: Number Magic
   #60: Picnic
   #61: Twin Cities

Chapter 7: Drama Games 93
   #62: Adverb
   #63: B-Movie Voice-Over Theater
   #64: Emotion Relay
   #65: Freeze
   #66: Hitchhiker
   #67: Please/No
   #68: Smile Gauntlet
   #69: Train Station/Bus Stop
   #70: Whopper
   #71: Wipe That Smile Off Your Face

Chapter 8: Group Builders 105
   #72: Clap On, Clap Off!
   #73: Freeway Follies
   #74: Hike in the Dark
   #75: Imagination Toss
   #76: Photographer
   #77: Suey, Suey
   #78: Timeline
   #79: Spot
   #80: Go With the Flow
   #81: Parting of the Sea

Chapter 9: High Energy 117
    #82: Wolf in Sheep's Clothing
    #83: Barnyard Hens
    #84: Everyone's "It" Tag
    #85: Hook 'Em
    #86: I'm Late, I'm Late, I'm Late …
    #87: Partners Tag
    #88: Spinning Wool
    #89: Tentacle Tag
    #90: Walking Tag

Chapter 10: General Silliness 127
    #91: Family Photo
    #92: Initial Success
    #93: Lamina Sign Language
    #94: Nine Birds
    #95: One Hen
    #96: One Noah's Ark
    #97: See a Psychiatrist
    #98: Belly Laugh
    #99: Story Jumble
    #100: Who's Knocking at My Door?
    #101: Hugs and Shrugs

Appendix A: Creating Your Own Programs 141
Appendix B: Games Chart 144
Appendix C: American Sign Language Alphabet 149
Resources for Recreation Leaders 150
About the Authors 152

Preface

We're honored that the first edition of this book sold out in just three years and that so many people have found it useful in leading others in recreation and ministry. It was adopted as a resource for the Logos program and has been selected as a text for college and seminary recreation courses.

This second edition provides clear instructions in a consistent format, some new games, and photographs for some of the games that are difficult to describe. We have also included variations of some tried-and-true favorites that have emerged through our own leadership of these games and some discussion starters for games that also serve as group-building activities.

We are honored that Healthy Learning has added this book to its line of "101" resources. We hope you'll find this updated second edition even more useful than the first. May you laugh lots as you learn and lead.

Introduction

Imagine this! The group members are laughing so hard they're crying, pointing, and shouting. They recount the past few minutes like they're old friends reminiscing. Gray hair, no hair, hair full of styling gel—they're together in the joy of the moment. For the moment, the cares of the world and time itself stand still.

Sometimes, fun like this just happens, but most of the time, fun is made intentionally. The people in the scene described aren't *old* friends. In fact, they just met 30 minutes before. An enthusiastic and skilled recreation leader has just guided them through a program of games and activities, and as a result, this group of strangers has become dear friends.

This is just one of many reasons for knowing a variety of games, for developing good recreation leadership skills, and for using recreation in many different areas of life. Recreation is *not* just something to fill up time during a lull in youth group or for those old folks at the nursing home who need some exercise. Instead recreation re-creates people. Coworkers find new ways to work together and solve problems; youth discover new skills and develop trust and leadership; strangers become friends; old and young find common ground in laughter.

More than this, those who play together discover that they can also pray together. The joy shared in moments of play creates a deeper sense of community—a sense of caring and common concern described by Paul in 1 Corinthians 12. Groups at play find that when one rejoices, all rejoice, and when one suffers, all suffer together as one unified body. In the laughter and the tears, groups suddenly become aware that they're in the presence of God.

This joy is a divine mandate! Jesus speaks to this when he said, "I said these things to you so that my joy may be in you, and that your joy may be complete" (John 15:11) and "Unless you … become like children, you will not enter the kingdom" (Matthew 18:3). Vulnerability, trust, laughter, crying, dependence on others, and freedom from the expectations of the world to be perfect can all surface and be embraced during an effective recreation experience.

Making Fun Out of Nothing at All is designed for those just beginning to lead recreation as well as seasoned veterans. It grew out of a need and desire to be able to lead effective recreation on the spur of the moment when Hula Hoops®, pantyhose, fun noodles, and other tools of the trade weren't available. You'll find in this collection of tested favorites and new crowd pleasers the tools you need to bring laughter and insight to your group.

We hope that as you use this resource God will use you as an angel to bring laughter and joy to God's children of all ages. We hope you and your groups will experience God laughing along with you.

How to Use This Book

This book contains 101 activities that can each be used to fill free time constructively, to set the mood for a program, or to simply have fun. Or you can combine them to create a complete recreation program that could fill an hour or more.

Each activity includes information to help you decide if it is appropriate for your group:
- *Objective:* This section briefly describes the preferred outcome of the activity.
- *Recommended Ages:* Most of the activities would be suitable for intergenerational groups, but a few work better with young children or youth and a few are really only appropriate for adults.
- *Number of Players:* Some activities work best with smaller groups of 20 or fewer, while others work better for much larger groups. Keep in mind that small group activities can be done with a large group if you have enough leaders to break the group into multiple small groups.
- *Energy Level:* Each game is rated 1 to 10 AMPS (Anticipated Moisture Perspired Scale). This gauge describes how much energy your participants will expend during the activity. A "1" is a quiet game, such as a mental teaser, while a "10" is highly aerobic and should come with a warning for anyone with heart conditions.

Other Features

The activities are grouped in the book according to categories, such as name games, circle games, mind teasers, etc. You can use several activities from the same chapter together or choose activities from different sections of the book. You can carefully compile your game list or you can randomly flip to a page to see if it fits your needs. This latter method has been known to be effective especially if you're leading a group that already knows each other and enjoys trying new things.

- Appendix A includes helpful advice for planning a custom program for your group and several sample programs for specific age groups.
- Appendix B includes a chart that cross-references the activities, allowing you to quickly find activities throughout the book that meet your goal for the group, such as names games, active games to burn lots of energy, or games appropriate for a specific age group, such as older adults.

Whatever the case, remember to have fun!

1

Top 10 Tips for Effective Recreation Leadership

Scenario 1: Your Middle Highs have gathered for their weekly youth fellowship meeting, and you receive a phone call that the scheduled speaker will be 45 minutes late. The kids have already gravitated to their cliques, some of the girls have retreated to the restroom, and others sit alone on stacks of chairs in various corners of the fellowship hall. You wonder if you can find a way to use this time to help the group bond.

Scenario 2: The board members or officers trickle into the conference room to start a new term, with a few stalwart vocal "pillars," a few new faces, and a larger percentage who are reluctant to make their opinions known. You wonder if this diverse group can become an effective and respectful team of decision-makers.

Scenario 3: The kids have finished their bag lunches, but the program for today's field trip isn't scheduled to begin for a while. You wonder if you can you keep these kids out of trouble in some way that's fun.

Scenario 4: The church has scheduled a family picnic, but the person who was responsible for recreation left all the sports equipment at home. You wonder if what activities you can do without this equipment that will help these families get to know each other better.

Using effective recreation leadership, you can answer all these questions with a resounding "Yes." The key word here is *effective*. Effective recreation leaders build groups, break down barriers, and help people have fun. Frequently, participants aren't even consciously aware that these positive things are happening. Effective recreation leaders are able to lead so people don't have to decide to participate. The leadership and the activities themselves are the invitation to join in and belong.

So, what makes a recreation leader effective? Here are 10 tips for success!

#1: Remember that whatever else you do, the goal is to have fun.

You can use recreation to help a group get to know each other better, to develop teamwork, and learn important things about themselves. However, if it isn't fun, chances are high that none of this is going to happen.

#2: "Do" your instructions whenever possible. Don't talk—do!

If your game involves a motion, a new prop, or a sound, show or tell the players how to *do* that first before explaining anything else about the activity. If a game is complicated, *do* the instructions in stages and build up to the goal. While an intellectual, left-brained leadership style has merit in some instances, participants often have trouble following lengthy instructions. The game may get delayed when you have to repeat directions or players may decide they don't like the game before it even starts.

Compare the following two leadership styles for the game "Catch the Leader":

Leader 1: Okay, group, we're going to play a game now called "Catch the Leader." I need everyone to stand in a circle, and we'll pick a volunteer to go out of the group who will come back and catch the leader. While that person's gone, we'll choose a leader and then we'll do everything the leader does. When the volunteer comes back, that person will stand in the center of the group and have three guesses to see if he can figure out who the leader is. When the volunteer succeeds, that person chooses the next person to go out of the circle.

Leader 2: Say "Everyone do this" and start clapping. Tell them to continue to clap while they get into a circle. Then say "Great! Now do what I do!" Start hopping on one foot, then wave, and then snap your fingers. Ask for a volunteer who's willing to leave the group for just a moment. When the first volunteer is gone, silently select a new leader and have the group follow the new leader. Call the volunteer back. Tell that person, "Stand in the center and see if you can guess who the leader is. Great! You did it! Now you pick someone else to go out of the circle!"

#3: Know that the first few activities will make or break the whole deal.

Make sure the very first activities are ones you know the group will enjoy. Plan to use activities you know are tried-and-true "winners" in order to set the pace; you can experiment later. It is generally *not* good to start your recreation time by saying," Well, I've never done this before, but let's see how this goes." The only exception is when you've worked with a group before and *everyone* knows what to expect from you as a leader.

#4: Know your group.

Most of the time, you'll work with familiar groups: your youth group, your church family, or your camper group. When choosing activities, take into consideration the abilities and interests of the group. For example, it makes much more sense to choose highly active tag games for children and more quiet and perhaps more cognitive activities for older adults. When selecting activities, it helps to know the answers to these questions:
- How many people will you have?
- What are their ages?
- Do they prefer a lot of activity or quiet mind-challenging games?
- What physical limitations need to be considered?

As your reputation as an effective recreation leader grows, you may find yourself asked to lead activities for groups you don't know. You'll be much more successful if you research the answers to these questions in advance.

#5: Know your schedule.

An effective recreation leader will choose activities that prepare the group for what's coming next. Maybe you've been frustrated as a leader when you were asked to lead Bible study right after a chaotic game of "Capture the Flag." If Bible study is next on the agenda, then close the recreation time with activities that are quieter and focus on the cognitive. While it's important to quiet folks down, it can be equally important to get folks "pumped up." If you're going to dig a ditch for Habitat for Humanity, then close with an activity that builds and energizes the group.

Before doing any recreation—spontaneous or planned—it's important to ask the following questions:
- How much time do you have?
- What do you want to do afterward?

#6: Whenever possible, plan ahead.

Planning can be remarkably hard for some leaders. Most effective recreation happens when the "flow" of the event is controlled by the leader. This usually happens best when the leader has a plan—written down if necessary. Plan more activities than you'll need. This way, you can change the plan as you go. Few things will kill the enthusiasm of participants faster than an unorganized leader who allows for lulls in activity.

A critical piece in planning for a lengthy recreation time is fitting activities into a "flow." Such a flow will result in making the participants feel comfortable and avoiding lulls in the transition between activities. (This is addressed more extensively in "How to Use This Book.") It's important to avoid a choppy program that moves back and forth between high-energy activities to quiet activities or goes from running to sitting to running again.

#7: Go with the flow and listen for the crescendo. Then, move on.

This is very important. Stop an activity when people are having the most fun and move on to something else. When you let an activity go "past its peak," participants will lose their focus and may want to quit before you're done. When they whine that they wanted more, you will know that you succeeded!

#8: Don't be afraid to play a game differently or change the plan in the middle.

If an activity isn't working like you hoped, either adapt it or move on to another game. If you're running out of time, pick the best game in your plan and close. Expect not to use all the games in your plan. Then, you can be flexible and be able to better meet your group's needs by playing what they want and need to play.

#9: Be enthusiastic. If you have fun, chances are the players will too.

Enthusiasm is contagious. The reverse is also true and can lead to disasters. If you don't have fun, the players almost certainly won't. You're the only one who can make good games better and difficult games fun.

#10: Practice, practice, practice.

Effective recreation leadership develops over time. Be reasonable in what you expect of yourself, and recognize that not every activity will go the way you hope, plan, or expect. Some great training events are listed in the resources section where you can get hands-on instruction and experience as a recreation leader. If you want to try something new, get a group of friends together and try it out before leading the game with the highly critical youth crowd or the reticent older adults. Until you feel confident, keep this book and your plan with you at all times.

Absolutely the most important key to effective recreation leadership is enjoying yourself and not taking yourself too seriously. We hope you find this resource an effective tool in developing your own leadership style.

2

Thou Shalt Play Safe: Avoiding the Seven Sometimes Deadly Sins of Recreation Leadership

Even more important than having fun is ensuring no one gets hurt during recreation. Children, youth, and parents should think of your camp, organization, or church as place where they can trust the leaders and the program. Unfortunately, it's so easy to get caught up in fun that potential problems can be overlooked.

Everyone makes mistakes. The professional learns from his mistakes as well as the mistakes of others. All the sins listed here have been committed by professionals. Read carefully and benefit from what others have already learned to avoid the same pitfalls.

#1: Make sure you remove hazards from your recreation space.

This is especially true if you're playing active games. Make sure there aren't any sharp objects people can run into, step on, trip over, etc. It's amazing what accidents can happen in a typical fellowship hall with leftover Christmas pageant decorations piled in one seemingly inconspicuous corner. Setting clear boundaries outdoors—such as "The stream is off limits"—and indoors—such as "You can only play in this half of this room"—can help you avoid disaster. When you're outdoors, take the time to remove downed limbs, sharp rocks, or other debris. You can even make a game of it and get your participants to help.

Is this serious stuff? Absolutely! A boy drowned at a camp when the boundaries were not clearly defined; he tried unsuccessfully to cross a raging stream to get an advantage in a game. Think through all the possibilities for danger before turning your charges loose to play.

#2: Never play games where anything is inserted in mouths or noses, and never allow someone to cover his mouth and nose.

There are too many cases where 911 has been called because someone stuffed 15 marshmallows in his mouth at once and choked. A player running with a toothpick in his teeth is asking for an accident. Discourage popular oldies such as bobbing for apples because of the potential for spreading infectious diseases.

At a workshop presented by one of the premier recreation publishers in the world, the leaders asked two volunteers to come forward without telling them what they'd be doing. The leaders put pantyhose over the volunteers' heads, covering their faces completely, and then covered the pantyhose in duct tape, adding more reversed duct tape so the sticky side was out. This was to be a "pocket scavenger hunt." The room was divided into two halves. A list of items was called out, and if an audience member had it with them, he was to stick it to his teammate's duct-tape-encased head. The list included coins, medicine, candy, etc. Once finished, the whole thing was cut off the heads of the now-dazed players and thrown into the trash.

This activity teaches a long list of things *not* to do (see #7), and the main point is this: If a participant doesn't die from an airway obstruction, the panic, injury, or embarrassment, then he may be turned off from recreation forever. The risks far outweigh any fun.

#3: Avoid games that are conducive to inappropriate contact—especially those that include sitting on laps.

Youth are already very self-conscious about their bodies, so don't ask them to play games where they may have to touch or be touched anywhere it could be uncomfortable. Who is doing the touching can also be an issue, such as the cute girl sitting on my lap or the ugly boy holding my hand. Participants should be thinking about how much fun they're having rather than worrying about issues such as these. For example, play the classic game "Sardines" with great caution. A bunch of people sandwiched into a small space can naturally lead to accidental (or not-so-accidental) inappropriate touching.

Tag games should have clear boundaries as to where on the body someone can and can't be tagged. Avoid activities in which objects touch inappropriate body parts. For example, in a popular relay, a string is passed through the clothing, including the underwear, of each participant.

A youth leader was charged with sexual misconduct because he regularly had one or more of the young ladies sit on his lap. Was it a game or was it something more? Don't put yourself or anyone else in that position.

#4: Remember that wrestling games, pillow fights, and some tag games often end because someone has gotten hurt.

These kinds of games need to be "adventure by choice." Don't pressure anyone into doing them or else simply avoid them altogether. You're trying to build group esteem; few things deflate a group faster than someone getting hurt. A classic example is "Capture the Flag." Many camps have stopped playing this game because of injuries and the arguments over who tagged whom. These games are also very hard to stop once a group gets riled up—especially older elementary or youth. Their competitive or aggressive spirit tends to bleed over into the next activities.

#5: Avoid any activity where the point is to embarrass or degrade someone and have fun at his expense.

A children's author and artist begins his presentation by doing a "portrait" of a volunteer without that person being able to see what's being drawn. The activity has nothing to do with the topic. Instead, the "portrait" is a degrading caricature intended to embarrass the volunteer and get a laugh, thereby breaking the ice with the audience.

#6: If you're leading any activity that involves physical or emotional risk, such as Challenge Course activities, be sure to get training first or invite a leader who's trained.

Far more injuries occur from so-called "low ropes" activities than those that are done 40 feet off the ground with safety equipment. Most of these injuries could have been avoided if the leader had been trained. In addition, some activities—if not debriefed properly—can leave participants feeling stupid or distrustful, therefore doing more harm than good. Training is available at many challenge courses and from organizations such as Project Adventure. Get trained if you want to lead these kind of adventure games.

This book offers three such activities for the benefit of those who have this training, and they're clearly labeled. Even with training, don't assume that everyone will enjoy or benefit from participating in these activities. Offer an alternative, such as being an active spotter or listener to help with the debriefing process.

#7: Don't use food as props or craft supplies. Avoid sending mixed messages.

In many churches, youth walk past the collection box for the local food pantry to some activity that uses food, such as covering people in peanut butter or making crafts with flour, beans, or macaroni. As long as starving people exist in this world, food isn't a toy.

Summary

Your participants will never know about your best planning because you provided them with a physically and emotionally safe environment for recreation. There are thousands of good and appropriate activities to choose from. Don't do anything that puts participants at unnecessary risk.

3

Mixers and Party Starters

#1: 15-Second Autobiography

Objective: To get to know three other people
Recommended Ages: 12 and up
Number of Players: 4 to 100
Energy Level: 2 AMPS
Formation: Standing in groups of four

Description:

- Players form huddles of four, with their heads in the center.
- Explain that each person in the huddle will tell his life story in 15 seconds.
- Choose someone to start (e.g., the tallest person, the person wearing the most blue).
- Have the starting player point to the person on his right, so each group knows which player speaks next.
- Give the signal to start, and after 15 seconds, yell "Switch!"
- The person on the right tells his life story in 15 seconds. Continue around the circle until everyone has told his life story.
- If you do not have a watch, you can count "One Biography, Two Biography, Three Biography," etc.

Leadership Tips:

- Some groups (especially younger ones) may need some suggestions before you start, such as "Tell your group your name, where you were born, your favorite hobby, where you go to school, what you want to be when you grow up, and the names of all your pets."
- Fifteen seconds may be too long for some groups. Yell "Switch!" when you hear the conversations beginning to lull.

#2: Amazing Adjective

Objective: To learn the names of everyone in the group
Recommended Ages: 8 and up
Number of Players: 5 or more
Energy Level: 1 AMPS
Formation: Sitting or standing in a circle

Description:

- Ask each person in the group to think about one adjective that best describes himself.
- Explain that the adjective needs to begin with the same letter or sound as his first name (e.g., Vivacious Vivian, Amazing Anthony, Silly Sarah, etc.).
- Each person repeats all the previous names and their adjectives and then adds his own adjective and name.
- To close the game, you the leader repeat everyone's adjective and name around the circle.

Leadership Tip:

- If the group is large, ask the participants to repeat only the adjectives and names of the three preceding players.

#3: Cliché Mixer Party Starter

Objective: To figure out the cliché or famous phrase
Recommended Ages: 10 and up
Number of Players: 6 to 30
Energy Level: 2 AMPS
Formation: "Clumps" of people (formed as they arrive)

Description:

- Before the group arrives, choose one, two, or three popular clichés. Try to match the number of people arriving to the number of words in a cliché or set of clichés. For example, if six people are due to arrive, use an expression such as "Every cloud has a silver lining." If someone fails to show, you can take the remaining word. If an extra arrives, that person can be a period, exclamation point, or quotation marks with you.
- When the first person arrives, give a warm greeting and say, "From now on, the only word you can say is *cloud*." (Do not give out the cliché's words in order.)
- Encourage players to greet one another with their words.
- Once everyone is present and you have given out all six words, announce that each person is a word in a popular cliché. Tell them to find the others in their group and to line up in order.

Leadership Tips:

- It's helpful to know how many are coming, although it isn't a requirement.
- Choose popular culture phrases, such as a line from a current commercial or movie, or a political catchphrase. Examples of well-known phrases are:
    ✓ "Put your money where your mouth is" (seven words).
    ✓ "Don't throw the baby out with the bathwater" (eight words).
    ✓ "The grass is always greener on the other side of the fence" (12 words).

#4: Get to Know You Marathon

Objective: To help people get to know each other
Recommended Ages: 6 and up
Number of Players: 2 to 50
Energy Level: 6 AMPS
Formation: Lined up on the starting line and facing the same direction

Description:

- Mark out a starting line and then have the players line up along it.
- Point out an imaginary line for players to cross that is about 10 to 20 yards from the group.
- Call out instructions to the players for their movement toward the goal. Use such instructions as "If you own a cat, take two hops forward"; "If you didn't take a shower this morning, take two steps back"; or "If you have jeans on, take three jumps."

Leadership Tips:

- Winning is not important in this game. In the next game, let the "winner" be a volunteer.
- Make up many different categories and motions, such as:
    ✓ "If you have a brother older than you, take one giant step."
    ✓ "If you went to church on Sunday, take 10 baby steps forward."
    ✓ "If you've ever been mountain climbing, shuffle two steps forward."
    ✓ "If you like to dance, dance forward five feet."

#5: Here I Sit in the Grass

Objective: To have some friendly competition while learning the names of group members

Recommended Ages: 5 and up

Number of Players: 8 or more

Energy Level: 6 AMPS

Formation: Sitting in a circle, with an open space to the left of the leader

Description:

- Teach the following three prompts:
    - ✓ Player #1: Here I sit…
    - ✓ Player #2: In the grass…
    - ✓ Player #3: With my friend, _____!
- Before starting, make sure to leave enough space for one player between you and the player to your left.
- Have Player #1 begin the game by saying "Here I sit" and then moving into the empty space.
- Have Player #2 say "In the grass" and then move into Player #1's vacated space.
- Have Player #3 say "With my friend, (name from someone else across the circle)!" and then move into Player #2's vacated space.
- Explain that the player just named by Player #3 now goes and sits in Player #3's vacated space, creating a new vacant space in the circle.
- Explain that the players on each side of the new vacant space will try to be the first to move into the new space.
- The winner of the space becomes the new Player #1 and begins the game again by saying "Here I sit." Continue to play as many rounds as you want.

Leadership Tips:

- This game is lots of fun outside, sitting in the grass as the name implies. It can be played indoors on the floor, or on a parachute, or in chairs.
- You can change the second line to "On the floor" or "In this chair" if desired.

#6: King Nebuchadnezzar

Objective: To learn names well enough not to get "caught"
Recommended Ages: 8 and up
Number of Players: 6 to 30
Energy Level: 3 AMPS
Formation: Sitting or standing in a circle

Description:

- Stand inside the circle.
- Point to someone in the circle and then say either "Right, good King Nebuchadnezzar" or "Left, good King Nebuchadnezzar."
- Explain that when you point at a player he should say the name of the person on his right or left before you finish speaking. If this player fails to state the correct name in time, he becomes the new pointer in the middle of the circle and continues the game.
- If the player says the name of the player on his right or left before you finish, point to someone else in the circle.

#7: Name Zoom

Objective: To learn the names of group members
Recommended Ages: 6 and up
Number of Players: 8 or more
Energy Level: 2 AMPS
Formation: Sitting or standing in a circle

Description:

- Say your name to the player on your right in the circle.
- Tell this player to say his name. Explain that everyone in the circle will say his name until all the names are passed around the circle and come back to you.
- Repeat this activity several times, increasing speed each time. To make it more challenging, try passing last names to the left around the circle.
- Super Challenge: Pass first names to the right and last names to the left at the same time!

Leadership Tips:

- If everyone already knows each other's names well, the word *zoom* can be substituted for the name so everyone is saying the same word. Then, pass the word *mooz* to the left.
- This activity can become a group builder if the leader asks between rounds for suggestions to improve performance. Time the group for speed; if no suitable watch is available, have a volunteer count seconds out loud.
- With a large group, two or more circles can compete against each other in a race. Have each group shout "Ta-da!" or another exclamation when it finishes.

#8: Partner Mixer

Objective: To get to know other group members
Recommended Ages: 6 and up
Number of Players: 10 to 100
Energy Level: 4 AMPS
Formation: Standing in a clump, moving to partners

Description:

- Tell the players to each find somebody born in a different month from themselves.
- Have the pairs shake their partners' hand. Explain that this is their "handshake partner."
- Encourage partners to exchange names and to find out as much about each other as possible. Suggest an opening question, such as "What is your favorite [food, movie, color, season, etc.]?"; "How many pets do you own?"; or "What is the most trouble you have ever been in?" This activity is very open-ended and can be tailored to fit your plan, group, setting, etc.
- You might want several different sets of partners for other activities you have planned. Give directions, such as "Now that you have found your partner, give that person a high five. This is your 'high-five partner.'"
- Tell the players to find new partners who like the same music they do.

Leadership Tips:

- In activities in which players select their own partners, it's always a good idea to have a "lost and found" area. If players haven't found a partner within 15 seconds, invite them to come to the lost and found area. Then, you can pair people whether or not they fit the category so no one is left out.
- This activity is great for getting a large group of people into partners, so the next activity (or even one later in the program) can be a partner game. At any point, you can tell them to find their high-five partner.
- Other "find a partner" cues include:
    - ✓ "Find somebody born in a state or country different from you."
    - ✓ "Find someone who belongs to a different church" (or school, team, etc.).
    - ✓ "Find somebody with the same color eyes as yours."
    - ✓ "Find a partner with a different shoe size from yours."
    - ✓ "Find someone who likes the same kind of books you do."
- Other handshake styles include:
    - ✓ Fist bump
    - ✓ Pinky swear
    - ✓ Low five

#9: Name-Dropper

Objective: To collect people from the other team while learning names
Recommended Ages: 8 and up
Number of Players: 10 to 50
Energy Level: 5 AMPS
Formation: Standing in two equal teams of players

Description:

- Have each team make a huddle that's far enough away from the other team that they can't hear what the other team is whispering.
- Ask each team to choose a player from its circle who will remain standing.
- Explain that when you yell "Drop!" both chosen players should point to each other as all the other team members kneel or squat.
- Tell the players that the first standing player who yells out the name of the other standing player wins that round for his team.
- Explain that the other standing player switches teams.
- The game continues until you're ready to move on to the next activity or all players have moved to the same team.

Leadership Tips:

- This game is best played with a group that has been together long enough to become acquainted. It's also a good game for integrating a few newer people into an already-established group.
- If the group is wearing nametags, have them remove them for this activity.

#10: Sound Effect Name Game

Objective: To learn the names of everyone in the group
Recommended Ages: 7 and up
Number of Players: 4 to 20
Energy Level: 1 AMPS
Formation: Sitting in a circle

Description:

- Invite the players to think about an exciting sound effect that begins with the same letter as their first name, such as "Pow! Pam," "Ka-Boom! Katie," "Alakazam! Anthony," or "Mmmmm! Mike."
- Ask the person to your right in the circle to tell his sound effect name. Explain that the next person repeats the first sound effect name and then adds his sound effect name.
- Each successive person on the right repeats all the names and then adds his name until everyone has given his sound effect name.
- You the leader close the game by saying all the sound effect names.

4

Group Games

#11: Aardvarks, Ducks, and Lambs

Objective: To claim a place in the circle and become an animal
Recommended Ages: 6 and up
Number of Players: 12 to 60
Energy Level: 9 AMPS
Formation: Sitting in a circle

Description:

- Select a volunteer to kneel in the center of the circle.
- Designate each player in the circle as an Aardvark, Duck, or Lamb. Tell the group to remain in that order. Be sure the circle has an equal number of each animal. The volunteer in the center has no animal designation yet.
- Tell the players that each animal group has its own unique way of traveling:
  - ✓ Aardvarks: Crawl across the circle with their noses to the floor while saying out loud as they travel, 'Sniff-sniff, sniff-sniff, sniff-sniff!"
  - ✓ Ducks: Waddle (i.e., walk in a squat), flap their wings, and "quack" loudly.
  - ✓ Lambs: Crawl on all four legs while saying "Baa! Baa!"
- Explain that the volunteer in the center will call out one of the three animal groups and that everyone in this animal group must move to a new spot in the circle.
- Tell everyone that after calling out an animal group, the volunteer in the center will move in the manner of the animal trying to reach one of the empty spots. The volunteer becomes whatever animal he called. (Remind the volunteer to become the animal just called, even if he's already been a different animal.)
- The person in the middle becomes the new volunteer, calls a different animal group, and play continues.

Leadership Tips:

- As leader, you either play or observe so the number of players in the circle will be divisible by three.
- This game requires a lot of crawling around on the floor, so it might be best to play this game with younger groups.
- To make this game a little less energy-intensive and a little more adult-friendly, play it standing and use the following motions:
  - ✓ Aardvarks: Walk across the circle, stick out their tongues, and say "Sniff-sniff."
  - ✓ Ducks: Quack loudly as they flap their wings.
  - ✓ Lambs: Use their hands to make floppy ears while saying "Baa! Baa!"

#12: Cliché Shout

Objective: To guess the cliché the other team has shouted
Recommended Ages: 10 and up
Number of Players: 12 or more
Energy Level: 2 AMPS
Formation: Two teams lined up facing each other, with about five feet between them

Description:

- Ask each group to secretly choose a cliché, such as "Every dog has his day." Assign one of the words to each player in the group. If you have more people than words, it's fine if two people have the same word. If you have more words in the cliché than people, assign just the key words. For example, with "You can catch more flies with honey than vinegar," you could assign "you," "catch," "flies," "honey," and "vinegar."
- Have the players line up in two lines facing each other.
- Select one team to go first. Explain that on your signal, all players on that team will say their assigned word at the same time.
- Explain the following rules: In the first round, the team to use a normal speaking voice to say the word and the listening team will guess the cliché. If they guess incorrectly, in the second round, the speaking team will shout their words and the listening team will guess again. If the guess is incorrect again, then the speaking team will whisper the words, and for the fourth and final time, the listening group gets to choose one of the three ways to hear the cliché again. If the cliché is not guessed this time, the other team gets to have a turn.

Leadership Tips:

- After each team has one turn, continue the play. Let the listening group pick how the cliché is spoken each time.
- This game works well as a drama exercise. Have the groups say their word in their best "stage whisper" (i.e., a voice that is spoken loudly but sounds like a whisper).
- Example clichés include:
    ✓ "If at first you don't succeed, try, try again."
    ✓ "The bigger they are, they harder they fall."
    ✓ "Better safe than sorry."
    ✓ "You can't have your cake and eat it too."
    ✓ "There's no such thing as a free lunch."
    ✓ "The check is in the mail."

#13: Echoes and Double Echoes

Objective: To get Player #2 to echo Player #1's one-syllable word
Recommended Ages: 10 and up
Number of Players: 2 to 100
Energy Level: 2 AMPS
Formation: Standing in pairs

Description:

- Have the group get into pairs and then select one partner of each pair (tallest, shortest, youngest, etc.) to go first.
- Explain that Player #1 will say words of two or more syllables, which Player #2 says like an echo. However, if Player #1 says a one-syllable word, the proper response for Player #2 is to reply by saying "Echo." If Player #2 remains silent or repeats back the one-syllable word, this is a victory for Player #1.
- Give the players some examples:
  Player #1: Computer
  Player #2: Computer
  Player #1: Airplane
  Player #2: Airplane
  Player #1: Hymn
  Player #2: Echo
  Player #1: Tiger
  Player #2: Tiger
  Player #1: Cat
  Player #2: Cat … Argh!
- After about a minute, yell "Switch!" Now Player #1 has to echo what Player #2 says.
- In Double Echoes, Player #1 gives only one-syllable words and Player #2 echoes with a word of two or more syllables that has a meaning similar to the original word.
- Give the players some examples:
  Player #1: Duck
  Player #2: Mallard
  Player #1: Stove
  Player #2: Burner
  Player #1: Dog
  Player #2: Canine

Player #1: Shoe

Player #2: ... (no answer for roughly three seconds—Player #1 wins this round)

Leadership Tips:

- This is a thinking game. It's best played when an upcoming activity requires mental alertness.
- This game can be very frustrating for some. It could lead to a discussion about not taking yourself too seriously or how to maintain composure in frustrating circumstances.

#14: Fast Math

Objective: To be the first person in a pair to add up the number of fingers
Recommended Ages: 8 and up
Number of Players: 2 or more
Energy Level: 2 AMPS
Formation: Partners facing each other

Description:

- Have the players get into pairs and then face each other with their hands behind their backs.
- Explain that when you give the signal, each partner will hold out one hand with any number of fingers extended. The first person to shout the total of the combined fingers wins that round.
- Have them play several rounds in quick succession.

Leadership Tips:

- Once the partners have mastered the additions, have them subtract the larger number from the smaller instead. (If both partners extend the same number of fingers, the round is a draw.)
- To make it even more difficult, tell them to multiply the number of the fingers.
- This game leads well into #15: Sign Language Shoot-Out or vice versa.
- Combine pairs into groups of four or six and then have them play a round adding up all the fingers in the group. This makes a good transition to a larger circle game.

#15: Sign Language Shoot-Out

Objective: To name an animal before your opponent
Recommended Ages: 7 and up
Number of Players: 2 to 200
Energy Level: 3 AMPS
Formation: Partners facing each other

Description:

- This is an excellent tool for teaching the American Sign Language alphabet.
- Have the players get into pairs. Demonstrate the first three letters of the American Sign Language alphabet.
- Tell each partner to hold one hand behind his back and face his partner.
- Explain that at your signal, both players are to quickly pull out their hand, showing an "A," "B," or "C." The first player to name an animal that begins with the *other* player's letter is the winner.
- Play several rounds.

Leadership Tips:

- The leader should also add more letters as time and the game warrant.
- This game leads well into #14: Fast Math or vice versa.
- By playing #8: Partner Mixer first, you can exchange partners easily by saying, "Great. Now go find your high-five partner and play again!"

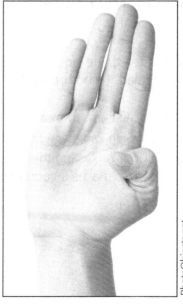

#16: Firecrackers

Objective: To not smile or laugh while being a firecracker
Recommended Ages: 8 and up
Number of Players: 10 to 40
Energy Level: 4 AMPS
Formation: Spread out inside the play area

Description:

- Select two or three volunteers to stand off to the side while you give the instructions.
- Ask the rest of the players to stand up straight and rub their hands back and forth in front of them as if it were a cold morning. Then, tell them to rub their hands together over their heads to pretend they're human firecrackers.
- Explain that it's the job of the volunteers (people standing off to the side) to extinguish the firecrackers by making a player laugh or smile. Tell players that the firecrackers may not close their eyes. The volunteers may not touch the firecrackers, but they can talk, sing, laugh, or gesture appropriately.
- Once extinguished, a firecracker then helps volunteers to extinguish other firecrackers.
- Explain that if you shout "Cover your ears," all firecrackers still burning are to make an exploding noise, such as "Ka-Blam!"

Leadership Tips:

- For young players especially, it's fun to practice the "explosion" before the game begins.
- Play several rounds so the initial volunteers have the opportunity to be firecrackers.

#17: Gossip/Physical Gossip

Objective: To communicate a phrase or picture from the first person to the last person
Recommended Ages: 8 and up
Number of Players: 5 to 50
Energy Level: 2 AMPS
Formation: Sitting in a straight line

Description:

- Whisper a phrase to the person at the one end of the line. Tell this person to whisper the phrase to the next person. Explain that each person in the line is to whisper the phrase only once and may not repeat any part of it or answer questions about the phrase.
- Once the last person in the line receives the phrase, ask her to say what she heard to the whole group. Have the group compare the statements by repeating what you said.
- Variation: In Physical Gossip, whisper to the person at the end of the line, telling him the name of a simple object to draw, such as a house, a star with five points, a star with six points, a tree, etc.
- Tell the player that the line is to do this until it reaches the first person. Ask that person to identify the object.

Leadership Tips:

- Both games can also be played while sitting in a circle.
- For a discussion about distractions, play the game twice. The first time, allow the players to talk among themselves while the phrase is being passed. The second time, ask them to be quiet until the last person receives the whispered phrase.
- Both games can be played in teams. After the first round, ask whether finishing first or being accurate was more important to the groups. Discuss how having "teams" can often create a competitive atmosphere, even if that isn't the goal.
- Both games can serve as helpful discussion starters on how easy it is to misunderstand or be misunderstood. Ask the group to identify ways to improve communication among the group.

#18: Without Anyone Else Knowing ...

Objective: To learn more about other members of the group
Recommended Ages: 10 and up
Number of Players: 6 to 100
Energy Level: 3 AMPS
Formation: Spread out and moving into a circle

Description:

- As each person arrives, explain that he is now a "spy" with a secret task to perform as he mingles with the crowd.
- For example, tell the person to do one of the following things (without anyone else knowing):
  ✓ Learn as many middle names as he can.
  ✓ Learn as many home states as he can.
  ✓ Find out who is a cat lover and who is a dog lover.
  ✓ Find out who voted in the last election.
  ✓ Find out who showered this morning.
  ✓ Find out who went to church this Sunday.
  ✓ Find out what the favorite deodorant of the group is.
- Once everyone has arrived and has had a chance to mingle for a few minutes, call the group together in a circle.
- Ask each person to come forward one at a time. Explain that it's the group's goal to figure out what kind of information each person was trying to gather. Once the group guesses, ask the "spy" to share what he discovered.

Leadership Tips:

- If a lot of people are due to arrive, select five or more spies and then ask the other guests to mingle and greet other people. Warn them that there are "spies" around trying to find out information.
- This is a great mixer to bring a group back together after a break.
- If the group has been focusing on a particular topic, gear the questions toward the topic. For example, if the group has just been studying first aid, have the spies find out who has broken a bone, ridden in an ambulance, or had an X-ray.

#19: Human Keyboard

Objective: To cooperatively spell phrases as a group
Recommended Ages: 10 and up
Number of Players: 20 or more
Energy Level: 4 AMPS
Formation: Standing in a circle

Description:

- Assign each person a letter in the alphabet.
- Have the players stand slightly bent, putting their hands on their knees.
- Explain that you will call out the letters of the alphabet and the player with the corresponding letter is to stand up straight and then move back into position while shouting his assigned letter. Let them practice.
- Then, shout out a silly word or sentence for the group to spell one letter at a time.

Leadership Tips:

- This is a good beginning activity for teamwork and cooperation.
- For groups smaller than 26, drop such letters as X, Z, Q, and J or have some players represent more than one letter.
- For more than 26 people, also assign "space," "period," "comma," and "exclamation point" to players.
- For larger groups, form two or more teams and then assigned letters. See which group can spell the phrase first.
- If you're fortunate to have 26 to 31 players, ask them to arrange themselves like the standard English ("Qwerty") keyboard. Then, ask them to "type" phrases. For more than 26, you will need to assign punctuation in this recommended order: comma, period, space, semicolon, and apostrophe.
- A sentence such as *The quick brown fox jumps over the lazy dog* includes every letter of the alphabet and, of course, every player. Trivia fun: A sentence that includes every English letter is called a *pangram*.) Some other examples include:
  ✓ The five boxing wizards jump quickly.
  ✓ Jinxed wizards pluck ivy from the big quilt.
  ✓ Amazingly few discotheques provide jukeboxes.
- If chairs are available, a lower-energy game can be played, allowing participants to sit and shout out the assigned letter. This makes the game more accessible and, therefore, fun for older adults and intergenerational groups.

#20: Spy

Objective: To correctly identify the spy

Recommended Ages: 8 and up

Number of Players: 10 or more

Energy Level: 4 AMPS

Formation: A tight circle, facing inward with eyes closed, with one hand extended backward out of the circle and the palm up

Description:

- Tell the players that the person whose palm is tapped twice will become the secret spy. Move around the circle, tapping each palm. Tap one palm twice and all others only once. After going around the circle, exclaim: "Eyes open—there's a spy among us."
- Tell everyone in the room to shake hands and greet each other. Explain that everyone must shake hands and can't refuse a handshake.
- Tell the spy to "tazer," or disable, players by using her right index finger to tap the wrist of the victim. Tell victims they're to take three or four more steps after being "tazered," possibly shake another hand, and then carefully fall down.
- Explain to the players that it's the goal of the spy to incapacitate everyone without being caught. If two players think they know who the spy is, tell them to join hands. Tell them to announce that they know who the spy is, giving the name of that person.
- If they're correct, the round ends; if they're not correct, have them sit silently while the round continues.
- At the end of the round, have the players sit in a circle again and then you can chose another spy.

Leadership Tips:

- You can also let the outgoing spy choose the next spy. This player will not shake hands with the group but will wait to determine if accusations about the spy are correct.
- Playing this game in the dark will increase the mystery. If you do that, make sure the space is clear of obstacles.

#21: Machine Charades

Objective: To act out a machine while other groups guess
Recommended Ages: 6 and up
Number of Players: 8 or more
Energy Level: 5 AMPS
Formation: Standing in equal groups of 10 people or fewer

Description:

- Ask each group to choose an everyday machine, such as a washing machine, computer, television, car, microwave, etc.
- Explain that they're going to act out the machine with their bodies.
- Give the groups about five minutes to prepare. Encourage each group to include every member of its group in the demonstration of its machine.
- Ask the groups to perform their machine one at a time. Invite the other groups to guess the machines.

Leadership Tips:

- Children always want to shout out their guesses before the group finishes its demonstration. Encourage players to wait until the performing groups shouts "Ta-da!" before they try to guess. It also helps to have an adult leader with each group for crowd control.
- Another variation of the game is to have the machines finish their demonstration by overheating and melting down.

#22: North and South

Objective: To switch partners without getting caught without a partner
Recommended Ages: 10 and up
Number of Players: 9 or more
Energy Level: 8 AMPS
Formation: Standing back to back in pairs around the play area

Description:

- Tell the pairs that they're to find out which partner was born the furthest north.
- Designate one direction of the play area as "north" and the opposite direction as "south." Have the person born furthest north face toward the designated "north" and his partner face toward designated "south."
- Have one person stand in the center alone. Explain that this person wants to get a partner and will shout either "north" or "south." If south is called, all the players facing south will run to find a new north partner and stand back-to-back. Tell players facing north not to move. If north is called, all players facing north should run and all players facing south should remain still.
- Explain that the person in the center will take the place of one of the players during the shuffle. The leftover player will become the new leader and will shout a direction to continue the play.

Leadership Tips:

- It's important that the player in the center become a member of the group she has called, even if she faced the opposite direction earlier in the game.
- If you have a lot of players, have them stand in back-to-back groups of four, facing all four directions, so the person in the center can also call out "east" or "west."

#23: Rain Dance

Objective: To create the sound of a thunderstorm
Recommended Ages: 5 and up
Number of Players: 5 or more
Energy Level: 3 AMPS
Formation: Standing or sitting in a straight row or circle

Description:

- Explain to players that they're going to make a rainstorm. Explain that when you pass directly in front of them, the players are to duplicate the motions and sounds you're making.
- As you walk in front of the group the first time, begin by rubbing your palms together. As you walk in front of the group again, gently snap your fingers. On the next pass, slap your legs and then clap your hands, building in volume as in a real rainstorm.
- To make the rain end, do the motions in reverse order: clapping hands, slapping legs, snapping fingers, rubbing palms, and then, finally, silence.

Leadership Tips:

- This is a wonderful activity for quieting a large group and preparing them to listen.
- If your group knows everyone well and is comfortable with touch, this is a great backrub activity. Have participants sit or stand in a circle—close enough to touch the back in front of them without reaching. Start with flat hands rubbing on the back, then scratch gently with fingertips, then tap with fingertips, then gently karate chop, and then pat with the full hand. Make the rain disappear by doing the motions in reverse order. This is a great way to end a day of hard physical or emotional work.

#24: Simon Says Time Warp

Objective: To follow one action behind "Simon"
Recommended Ages: 7 and up
Number of Players: 10 to 100
Energy Level: 6 AMPS
Formation: Standing and facing the leader

Description:

- Remind everyone of the rules for the traditional Simon Says. Tell them that in that game, the leader will give directions, such as: "Simon says put your hands on your head"; "Simon says touch your toes"; "Simon says pat your stomach."
- Explain that in this version, the players will only follow the leader's instructions after he has given the next instruction. Give the following example:
  Leader: Simon says put your hands on your head. (Players should do nothing.)
  Leader: Simon says touch your toes. (Players should put their hands on their heads.)
  Leader: Pat your stomach. (Players should touch their toes.)
  Leader: Simon says run in place. (Players should continue touching their toes.)

Leadership Tips:

- This game is best played just for fun, with no one being eliminated. The energy level can be whatever the leader chooses.
- If played as an elimination game, have players move to a second game being played at the same time, such as #25: Simon Says Swap.

#25: Simon Says Swap

Objective: To play a no-elimination variation of the traditional Simon Says
Recommended Ages: 8 and up
Number of Players: 10 to 100
Energy Level: 6 AMPS
Formation: Standing in two groups, each facing a different leader

Description:

- Play this game by using two leaders who already know the traditional version of Simon Says.
- Have each group follow its own leader in the traditional game of Simon Says.
- When players in either group are "caught," they are to move to the other group.
- Explain that in this version, no one is ever "out." Encourage them to try to get all the players into one group or the other.

#26: Singing Charades

Objective: To figure out song titles acted out by volunteers
Recommended Ages: Any
Number of Players: 6 or more
Energy Level: 3 AMPS
Formation: Two groups of equal players

Description:

- Invite someone from each group to get the name of a song from you.
- Have the player return to the group and act out the title of the song in typical charades fashion.
- Explain that the first group to begin singing the correct song is the winner of that round.
- After each round, have another volunteer get a new song.

Leadership Tips:

- Choose songs everyone will know, such as children's songs, patriotic songs, popular songs currently airing, or songs specific to your group.
- Start with simple songs, such as "Row, Row, Row Your Boat," and then build to more difficult ones.
- If you get tired thinking of songs, have the group that has figured out the least number of songs chose someone to become the new leader for this game.

#27: Statues

Objective: To figure out which player is the "secret statue"
Recommended Ages: 8 and up
Number of Players: 7 to 30
Energy Level: 3 AMPS
Formation: Standing apart in the playing area

Description:

- Tell everyone to pretend they're statues and to strike a pose.
- Ask for a volunteer to come forward. Tell that player to watch the players as they make statue poses. Then, have the volunteer face away from the group and spell the word *statues* out loud. During this time, slightly change one statue's pose.
- Ask the volunteer to turn around and then guess the statue that has changed. Allow about 10 seconds for the volunteer to make a guess.
- If the volunteer guesses correctly, the statue becomes the guesser and you select a new statue. If the guess isn't correct, have the volunteer turn away and spell *statues* again. During this time, the statue changes his pose even further.
- Give the volunteer three tries (i.e., a total of three guesses). After three unsuccessful guesses, choose a new volunteer and begin play again.

Leadership Tips:

- Because good recreation leaders want their volunteers to be successful, give hints to the guesser or adjust the "secret statue" so the statue is obvious on the third try.
- With certain age groups, you may need to remind the group to be respectful in their poses. Be clear that inappropriate poses aren't allowed.

#28: Thumb Grab

Objective: To catch another player's thumb while not letting your own thumb get caught
Recommended Ages: All
Number of Players: 2 to 100
Energy Level: 3 AMPS
Formation: Standing in pairs

Description:

- Demonstrate the hand positions. Make a loose cup with your left hand, large enough to fit someone's thumb. Make a fist with your right hand, with the thumb extended toward the floor.
- Ask everyone to face their partners. Tell them that everyone's left hand should form the cup and that everyone's right thumb should point toward the ground.
- Tell the players to place their right thumb into their partner's left hand "cup."
- Explain that on the count of three, each player is to try and remove his thumb while at the same time holding onto his partner's thumb.
- Count to three—and then let the laughter begin.

Leadership Tips:

- As the leader, demonstrate one round with a partner before asking the players to make the hand positions.
- Usually, three rounds of this game is perfect.
- After successfully playing the game with partners, have two sets of partners join to make a group of four facing each other in a square. Have each person hold out his left hand to the left in the cup shape and put his right-hand thumb down and into the cup formed by their neighbor's left hand. Count to three and then let the grabbing and laughter begin. Continue to double the size of each group until the whole group is one large thumb-grabbing circle.
- An alternative hand combination is to place the inverted thumb on the partner's open palm When the signal is given, each player tries to grab the thumb with the outstretched hand. Some players find this even more difficult. It may be more appropriate for some groups.

#29: Touch Twister

Objective: To engage the group in nonthreatening, silly touch
Recommended Ages: 6 and up
Numbers of Players: 8 or more
Energy Level: 4 AMPS
Formation: Standing as a group in a close clump

Description:

- Invite the group to get close together in a clump.
- Give such instructions as "Reach out with your right hand and touch something green on somebody else" or "Reach out with your right hand and touch someone else's ear."
- Tell players to keep their right hand in place as you give other instructions. Use the following example as a model:
    - ✓ With your right hand, reach out and touch something red on somebody else.
    - ✓ With your left hand, reach out and touch something metal on somebody else.
    - ✓ With your right foot, reach out and touch someone else's knee.
    - ✓ With your nose, reach out and touch someone else's shoulder.

Leadership Tips:

- You need to know your group well for this game. Be careful to avoid any unwanted or immature touching. The simple clarification "Remember to be ladies and gentlemen" can go a long way with adolescents.
- For groups with mobility issues, have players do one instruction at a time. The modified instruction would be like this: "With your left hand touch something metal on someone else. Let go with your right hand."

#30: Two-Team Spelling Bee

Objective: To guess a seven-letter word

Recommended Ages: 10 and up

Number of Players: 9 to 30

Energy Level: 3 AMPS

Formation: Standing in a group of seven, with the remaining players divided into two teams

Description:

- Ask the group of seven players to form a tight huddle and quietly select a seven-letter word. Have the players assign one letter of that word to each person in that group.
- Divide the remaining players into two teams and then have the group of seven line up in front of them.
- Tell each person in the group of the seven to shape his body as closely as possible to his assigned letter and remain frozen in that pose. Explain to the group of seven that they're to scramble the letters so they don't spell out the word they chose.
- Explain that the teams are to taking turns asking one letter to move somewhere else so they can make a guess.
- Tell everyone that the goal is to be the first team to correctly guess the word on its turn.

Leadership Tips:

- Players are allowed to tell the teams the letter they represent if there is confusion.
- If 21 or more people are present, divide them into three teams, with each team performing a word.
- For younger people or smaller groups, use words with only five or six letters.

5

Circle Games

#31: About-Face

Objective: To get a new spot in the circle without getting caught in the middle
Recommended Ages: 8 and up
Number of Players: 20 to 100
Energy Level: 8 AMPS
Formation: Standing in a circle

Description:

- Have the players stand in a circle, with a player or leader in the center. Instruct every other player to face outward so half the group is facing into the circle and half are facing out. Have all the players in the circle hold hands.
- Tell the person in the center to yell out a color. Tell the players facing into the circle who are wearing that color to drop hands, run to a vacant spot in the circle, and join hands again. The vacant spots are marked by the players facing outward who don't run. Tell players that it's the goal of the person in the center to jump into a vacant spot, leaving another player in the center.
- Explain that every time a new player enters the center, he will say "About-face!" as a signal for all the players in the circle to turn to face the opposite direction. Then, instruct the new center person to yell out a color, and play will begin again.

Leadership Tips:

- This is a way to play classic "turnover" games in which players race for a new spot in a circle.
- To keep the circle an even number, you can play or not play.
- This game works best if you practice the about-face turn a few times before playing the game by switching places.
- The person in the center can use any number of categories, such as birth months, states they've visited, years in school, eye color, etc.

#32: Anatomy Lesson

Objective: To confuse a member of the group

Recommended Ages: 4 and up

Number of Players: 4 to 30

Energy Level: 3 AMPS

Formation: Seated or standing a circle, with a volunteer or the leader in the center of the circle

Description:

- Have the person in the middle select another player in the circle. He points to one of his own body parts while saying the name for another body part. For example, "This is my knee" while pointing to his elbow or "This is my chin" while pointing to an ear. The selected player has a count of 10 to point to the named body part while saying the part that was pointed to. For example, "This is my elbow" while pointing to his knee or "This is my ear" while pointing to his chin.
- If the response is correct, the player in the center selects another person in the circle and the game continues. If the correct response isn't given within the count of 10, the two players trade places.
- The new player in the center then tries to confuse someone else.

Leadership Tips:

- It's a good idea to demonstrate a few rounds as the leader in the center before beginning with a volunteer.
- The person in the middle may need to be reminded to count to 10.
- Certain age groups may need to be reminded to be ladies and gentlemen as this game is played, but it does work well with all ages.

#33: Are You the Spy?

Objective: To race another player around the circle and be the first to claim the one open spot
Recommended Ages: 8 and up
Number of Players: 12 to 50
Energy Level: 8 AMPS
Formation: Standing in a close circle, holding hands and facing inward

Description:

- Ask a volunteer "detective" to stand in the center with his eyes closed.
- Silently choose a person in the circle to be the "spy." Once you've chosen the spy, instruct the detective to begin asking players, "Are you the spy?"
- Tell the players that they should answer "No." Tell the person who is the spy to say nothing when he's asked and to drop the hands he's holding.
- Tell the two players on the right and left of the spy to leave the circle and race around the circle in opposite directions. As they race, explain that the detective will take one of the open spaces and join hands with players in the circle. The first player will claim the remaining open space and the second person back becomes the new detective.
- While the new detective closes his eyes, silently choose a new spy and then begin the play again.

#34: Big Bunny

Objective: To become the Big Bunny by not missing your turn
Recommended Ages: 8 and up
Number of Players: 10 to 50
Energy Level: 6 AMPS
Formation: Sitting in a circle

Description:

- Explain that you are the Big Bunny. Tell the group that the player to your immediate left is Little Bunny and the player to your immediate right is Number One, the player to his right is Number Two, and so forth, counterclockwise around the circle. Teach them the following chant and then let them practice a few times:

  Big   (hit your knees)
  Bunny (clap your hands)
  Big   (hit your knees)

Bunny	(clap your hands)
Big	(hit your knees)
Bunny	(clap–knees–clap)
Uh	(knees)
Huh	(clap–knees–clap)
Big	(knees)
Bunny	(clap–knees–clap)

- After the group has learned the rhythm (knees–clap–knees–clap), explain that from here on, the players are to call out their number position and a different number or "Little Bunny" or "Big Bunny" (instead of repeating "Big Bunny" throughout the chant), trying not to miss a beat. As a demonstration round, have the players call the numbers in sequence so everyone gets the chance to try the chant and keep it going. Big Bunny would begin the opening chant and start the round with "Big Bunny, Number One," "Number One, Number Two," "Number Two, Number Three," "Last Number, Little Bunny."
- Tell the group that if a player breaks the chant, that person becomes the new Little Bunny and moves to the spot immediately to the left of the Big Bunny. The player to the right of the vacant space moves into it and gets the next lower number, thus moving one space closer to the coveted Big Bunny position. Remind them that their goal is to become Big Bunny.
- Give them the following example of how a group can mess up:
  Big Bunny: "Big Bunny, Number Ten"
  Number Ten: "Number Ten, Number Two"
  Number Two: "Number Two, Number One"
  Number One: "Number One, Big Bunny"
  Big Bunny: "Big Bunny, Little Bunny"
  Little Bunny: "Little Bunny, Number One"
  Number One: "Huh, I missed. I wasn't paying attention."
- Explain that in this example, Number One would become the new Little Bunny and everyone else would move one spot closer to the Big Bunny. Tell everyone that once they've moved, Big Bunny begins again with the original chant.

Leadership Tips:

- This is a wonderfully fun, silly, and high-energy game that depends on the leader being able to teach a simple chant.
- Players soon learn to chant numbers lower than their own. They will find that nothing is better than catching the Big Bunny not paying attention when *everyone* moves one seat forward.
- This game adapts well to seasonal parties; for example, you may want to try Big Santa, Big Pumpkin, or Big Pilgrim.

#35: C'mon

Objective: To become the leader by wrestling your way to tag the current leader
Recommended Ages: 18 to 30
Number of Players: 12 or more
Energy Level: 10 AMPS
Formation: Sitting in two concentric circles

Description:

- Tell players in the inner circle to sit cross-legged between the raised knees of their partner in the outer circle. Have the players in the outer circle sit with both their palms on the floor.
- Explain that a player in the center will give one or more of the pairs the "c'mon" signal with his index finger.
- Tell the group that before giving the signal for the action to begin, the center person may call out one of the following three moves, which will mix the current partners:
    ✓ Switch: Front and back partners switch places.
    ✓ Right: Inner circle players move one person to the right.
    ✓ Left: Inner circle players move one person to the left.
- Once the center person gives the "c'mon" signal to a pair, tell the inner circle partner to try to tag the center person and the outer circle player to try to hold his partner back in order to protect the person in the middle.
- Explain that the inner circle player who succeeds in breaking free and touching the center person becomes the new center person for the next round.

Leadership Tips:

- This game is recommended only for adults. There is a risk of minor injury and accidental inappropriate touching. Players should be informed of the risks, and participation should be optional.
- Know your group. This game is only for groups with a very high level of trust and appropriate sense of friendly competition.

#36: Catch the Leader

Objective: To figure out who the leader is
Recommended Ages: 5 and up
Number of Players: 5 to 20
Energy Level: 6 AMPS
Formation: Standing or sitting in a circle

Description:

- Select a volunteer and then send that person away from the group. Choose a leader who will lead the group through various motions, such as hand clapping, finger snapping, whistling, hopping on one foot, etc. Explain that the players in the circle imitate the leader.
- Tell the players that the leader will keep switching activities. The task of the volunteer who left the circle is to figure out who the leader is.
- Once the group is engaged in the first motion, call the volunteer back to the center of the circle. He gets three guesses to figure out the leader.
- Explain that the first leader becomes the next volunteer and steps away from the group while a new leader is chosen.

Leadership Tip:

- After two guesses, encourage the leader to grossly exaggerate the motions to help the volunteer succeed.

#37: Categories

Objective: To name an item in the designated category faster than the volunteer can count to 10

Recommended Ages: 6 and up

Number of Players: 4 or more

Energy Level: 2 AMPS

Formation: Sitting or standing in a circle, with a volunteer in the center

Description:

- Explain that the volunteer will point to a person in the circle and say a category of grocery store items, such as cereal, bread, frozen pizza, etc. The selected person needs to give the brand name of a matching item before the volunteer can count to 10.
- Tell the group that if the volunteer reaches 10 before the brand is named, the players trade places and play continues. Otherwise, the volunteer points to a new person in the circle and shouts a new category.

Leadership Tips:

- You can use categories other than store items, such as: Bible characters, places, or books; historical figures or places; celebrities; TV shows or movie genres; cartoons; etc.
- If you're doing a party based on a theme, you can create categories to match that theme.

#38: Considering Cap

Objective: To advance to the "head" of the circle
Recommended Ages: 6 and up
Number of Players: 6 or more
Energy Level: 5 AMPS
Formation: Sitting, squatting, or kneeling in a circle

Description:

- Explain that this game depends on the leader and the group memorizing the following lines:

    Leader: The king has lost his considering cap and doesn't know where to find it. Some say this, some say that, some say Number Six has it.

    Number Six: Who, sir? Me, sir?

    Leader: Yes, sir. You, sir.

    Number Six: No, sir. Not I, sir.

    Leader: Then, who, sir?

    Number Six: Number One has it.

    Leader: Number One, go to the foot.

- Teach these lines to the group, having them repeat after you the "number" parts. Have the players count off and remember their number. Ask the players to move to a new position in the circle so the numbers are mixed up.
- Once players are seated in a new order, state that the person on your right is the "head" and the person on your left is the "foot." Explain that long ago, when kings would hold court, their most trusted advisers would be at the king's head and the least trusted advisers would be at the king's foot. Naturally, everyone would want to be in the king's favor and be as close to the head as possible.
- Begin the play by reciting the chant and ending with a number you select. For example: "… Number Two has it. Number Two, go to the foot."
- Tell Number Two to jump up and say, "Who, sir? Me, sir?' before the king can finish saying "Number Two, go to the foot."
- If Number Two succeeds in getting up in time, he proceeds with the chant and accuses some other number. If a king beats Number Two by finishing the statement, Number Two leaves his place in the circle and goes to sit at the king's left. Everyone sitting to the right of Number Two now advances one place closer to the king's head.

Leadership Tips:

- If you're fortunate to have someone you can teach in advance to join in the demonstration, this helps the players understand their lines and the flow of the game.

- It may be easiest to teach only these two lines: "Who, sir? Me, sir?" and "No, sir. Not I, sir." Have the players recite these several times before explaining the game.
- Play the first few rounds in slow motion so the participants have an opportunity to get comfortable with the lines.
- The king can assist the players in advancing by repeatedly calling the numbers of players who are seated close to the "head."
- The leader may choose to have the left be his head and the right be his foot just to keep experienced players guessing.
- This game can go on for hours, and there are children willing to play it for hours. The effective leader will move on to a different activity before players begin to lose interest. If someone is particularly good in the role of the head, the goal can become simply to catch that one individual.

#39: Countdown

Objective: To cooperatively count down to zero
Recommended Ages: 8 and up
Number of Players: 8 to 25
Energy Level: 2 AMPS
Formation: Sitting in a circle

Description:

- Explain that in this game, the players will count backward similar to the way people count down for a rocket blastoff. Tell players that the number you will start with equals the total number of players in the group.
- Begin the game by announcing "Commence countdown." Tell the players that they're to try to count backward to zero one player at a time without anyone being assigned a certain number and without anyone gesturing or talking except for the numbers.
- Explain the two rules:
  ✓ Players may not speak at the same time.
  ✓ Players may not speak when sitting beside someone who has just spoken.
- Tell the players that means that if either of these rules is broken, you will announce "Cancel countdown" and the group will need to begin again with the highest number.

Leadership Tip:

- While this game can be played just for fun, it also makes for a good teambuilding exercise. Ask the group to figure out what they did to complete the task successfully.

#40: Cross Your Palms

Objective: To build group cooperation and personal concentration by tapping hands on the floor in a particular order

Recommended Ages: 5 and up

Number of Players: 5 to 20

Energy Level: 5 AMPS

Formation: Kneeling in a circle and touching the floor with their palms

Description:

- Instruct each person to cross his right hand over the left hand of the person to his right, keeping all palms on the floor. All the players should now have their hands crossed over (or under) the hand of the people on both sides of them.
- Tell the group to begin by tapping the floor in order of the hands around the circle. Have the person to your right begin. Many players will lose track of which hands are their own—this is part of the fun.
- Rev up the game by reversing the direction or by telling players to tap only every other palm.
- After a while, tell players that any player can reverse the direction of the taps by tapping the floor twice.

Leadership Tips:

- If you know your group well and believe that no will have their feelings hurt, you can play this as an elimination game. When a person misses once, he must remove one hand from the circle; if he misses twice, he's eliminated. Encourage players who are eliminated to begin their own game nearby.
- Use a large round table to make this game more adult-friendly.

#41: Eye Contact

Objective: To successfully make eye contact with another player
Recommended Ages: 8 and above
Number of Players: 8 to 30
Energy Level: 5 AMPS
Formation: Standing in a tight circle

Description:

- Ask players to look at the floor and think about another person in the circle.
- Explain that when you tell them to look up, they should stare at the person they thought about.
- If two players are looking directly at each other, tell them to scream wildly, run from the circle, and embrace or join hands. When this happens, instruct the rest of the players to tighten up the circle.
- Keep the game moving by repeating only two instructions: "Look down!" and then "Look up!"
- Tell the players who leave the circle that they can begin their own game or remain with their partner in preparation for the next game.

Leadership Tips:

- Laughter is almost always a result of this game.
- Have the group practice the group scream—"Aaaaaah!"—before the first round. That can help participants feel more comfortable with screaming when it's their turn.
- With a group that's just forming in which names are still unfamiliar, ask the players to look at another's shoes when they look down and then look at that person when they look up. This can also help for younger children.
- This game is an excellent method of selecting partners for the next game.

#42: Gotcha

Objective: To catch players in the act of moving from a standing position to lying down

Recommended Ages: 6 to 40

Number of Players: 5 or more

Energy Level: 7 AMPS

Formation: Groupings of five or six players, with a volunteer in the center

Description:

- Explain that the goal of the players in the circle is to lie down on the floor without the person in the middle catching them as they move.
- Have the players in each circle spread out so each has enough room to lie down in his spot without touching or kicking another player. Give them the hint to lie down gradually and silently.
- Explain that the goal of the person in the center is to spot a player in motion. Tell them they're to point and yell "Gotcha!" whenever they see motion. Any player who's caught in motion has to return to a standing position and begin again. If a player makes it to the floor without being caught, that person becomes the new player in the center.

#43: Just Like

Objective: To encourage creativity and learn about other members of the group
Recommended Ages: 7 and up
Number of Players: 5 to 50
Energy Level: 1 AMPS
Formation: Sitting in a circle

Description:

- Ask each player to think about one item. It can be anything in the entire world.
- Begin by asking the person on your left to tell what his item is. Then, announce your item. Explain how your item is "just like" the other person's item.
- Tell the person on your right to state his item and to explain how it is "just like" your item.
- Explain that each player around the circle will name his selected item and how it is "just like" the item of the player sitting on his left until everyone has taken a turn.
- Examples include:
  Person on the left: Pencil.
  Leader: My car is "just like" a pencil because it moves like lead.
  Mike: My cucumber is "just like" a car because they both roll downhill.
  Joshua: My opossum is "just like" a cucumber because they're both "good eatin'."

Leadership Tip:

- Help the first few players as a demonstration. Once they've gotten the concept, ask them to think about new items and then begin again.

#44: Noah's Ark

Objective: To be alert enough to move to "Noah's" right hand
Recommended Ages: 6 and up
Number of Players: 6 to 30
Energy Level: 5 AMPS
Formation: Sitting in a circle

Description:

- Ask participants to pick an animal that might have been on Noah's Ark and then create a sign or gesture to go with that animal. For example, a gorilla would beat his chest, a bat would flap his wings, an elephant would raise his trunk, etc.
- Go around the circle and have players tell their animal and show their animal signs or gestures to the group.
- Tell the group you're Noah and then show a sign or gesture for Noah, such as drawing a rainbow in the air.
- Do your sign or gesture and then make someone else's animal sign or gesture. Explain that the person whose sign or gesture you did will now repeat their animal sign or gesture and then do someone else's.
- Have the group continue this pattern until one animal is caught "sleeping." Tell this player to get up and move to Noah's left. Tell the people to the right of the vacant space to move over one spot closer to Noah's right. The trick is to catch the animal sleeping that is just to the right of Noah so everyone has to move.

Leadership Tips:

- This game is similar to the games #34: Big Bunny and #49: What's Your Sign?
- You can also have the player make an animal sound to go with its motions. For example, a gorilla might beat its chest and say "Oo oo, ah ah," a lion might shake its mane and roar, a bat might flap its wings and squeak, etc.
- You can play the game silently, which makes paying attention crucial. This game can then be a good lead into an activity that requires attention.

#45: One Frog

Objective: To see how many frogs can be counted
Recommended Ages: 8 and up
Number of Players: 5 or more
Energy Level: 2 AMPS
Formation: Sitting in a circle

Description:

- Teach the players this repeating chant. Tell them it will require them to do a little math.
  One frog
  Two eyes
  Four legs
  In a pond
  Kerplunk
  Two frogs
  Four eyes
  Eight legs
  In a pond
  In a pond
  Kerplunk
  Kerplunk
  Three frogs
  Six eyes
  Etc.
- Have the players send this chant around the circle by saying one phrase per person. Encourage them to go as high as their brains will allow.
- Explain that they can't give each other verbal cues. You can also decide not to permit visual help.
- Tell the players to remember two important facts:
  - ✓ The number of body parts is always multiplied by the number of frogs.
  - ✓ "In a pond" and "kerplunk" are always repeated the same number of times as the number of frogs. For example, for one frog, say "kerplunk" once; for two frogs, say "kerplunk" twice; and so on.
- Tell the players they can play just to see how far they can go without someone goofing or they can set a specific goal, such as five frogs.

Leadership Tips:

- If the group is large, divide it into smaller groups and play as a race to five frogs or more, with each group having to start over if it goofs up.
- Use the game as a teambuilding exercise. Invite discussion about the "pressure to perform" and how that affects the group. Encourage them to discuss how it feels to be the one who goofs up and what team members can do to support each other when mistakes happen.

#46: Spontaneous Zoo

Objective: To make pictures on command
Recommended Ages: All
Number of Players: 6 or more
Energy Level: 6 AMPS
Formation: Standing or sitting in a circle

Description:

- Explain that players will work together to make pictures with their bodies. Tell them that a leader in the center will name a picture and three designated players will have until a count of 10 to assume the correct positions.
- Teach the following picture positions to the players:
    - ✓ *Elephant:* The middle person links his fingers together and makes the hanging-down trunk. Players on the left and the right of the trunk make big Cs with their arms and lean toward the middle person to make ears.
    - ✓ *Seal:* The middle person looks up and makes a large circle with both arms to form an imaginary ball on the seal's nose. The person on the right sticks out his right palm and the person on the left sticks out his left palm. Together, these two players will clap their hands together like flippers.
    - ✓ *Giraffe:* The middle person makes a long neck with both arms. Players on either side put their palms on the floor to make four legs. Sound: "Munch, munch, munch."
    - ✓ *Jellyfish:* The middle person puts both arms on top of his head, with his elbows sticking out parallel to his shoulders. Players on either side wave both their arms in front like tentacles.
    - ✓ *Scorpion:* The middle person puts both arms behind his head, with one hand on top of the other and his fingers extended. The player to the right makes a snapping pincher in front with his right hand and the player to the left does the same with his left hand.
    - ✓ *Monkeys:* Three players take the "see no evil, hear no evil, speak no evil" positions by covering their eyes, ears, and mouth in order.
    - ✓ *Raging Viking:* The players on the left and the right make horns on the "helmet" of the middle person by making a Y in American Sign Language with their hands. The middle person screams out a war cry.
    - ✓ *Spirit of '76:* Like the classic painting, the person in the middle plays the drum, the person on the right holds up the flag, and the person on the left plays the fife.

- Encourage players to make the noises associated with these pictures.
- Once you have taught the positions, explain that the leader in the center will point to a player in the circle, name a picture, and begin to count to 10. The player at whom the leader pointed is the middle person. If any of the three players fails to form a portion of the picture before the count of 10, he becomes the new leader in the center.

Leadership Tips:

- Begin with one or two simple pictures and then add the more difficult pictures as you go.
- Keep the game fresh by inventing new pictures of your own. Be creative!

#47: This Is an Eagle

Objective: To "pass" an eagle in one direction around the circle and a "porcupine" in the opposite direction at the same time
Recommended Ages: 5 and up
Number of Players: 5 or more
Energy Level: 2 AMPS
Formation: Sitting in a circle

Description:

- First, teach the two hand motions for the "eagle" and "porcupine":
  - ✓ Eagle hand motion (Figure A): Hook thumbs together, with palms facing in, and flap the other eight fingers.
  - ✓ Porcupine hand motion (Figure B): Interlock all the fingers and then extend eight fingers, with the thumbs down.
- Begin by making the eagle hand motion and showing it to the person to your right (Player #1). Say, "This is an eagle." Explain that this player (#1) is to respond by saying, "A what?" Answer back by saying "An eagle" while making the eagle motion.
- Tell the player on your right (#1) to turn the player on his right (#2), make the eagle motion, and say, "This is an eagle." Explain that that player (#2) will respond, "A what?" However, tell them that #1 will not answer the question but will turn to you and ask you "A what?" You will say "An eagle" to #1, who will then say "An eagle" to #2.
- Explain that this pattern will continue. Player #2 will turn to the next person in the circle and say, "This is an eagle" and the question "A what?" will travel back to you each time, and your answer "An eagle" with the hand motion will then travel back to the asker.
- Let them practice for a while until everyone understands the pattern.
- Tell them that now it's time to begin the game for real. Explain that you will pass the eagle to your right around the circle (Figure C) and you will pass the porcupine to your left around the circle (Figure D).
- Let the fun begin—particularly when the two signs pass each other on the far side of the circle.

Leadership Tips:

- This game is pure silliness; help players not to take it too seriously.
- Encourage players to continue with the hand motions as play moves around the circle, as this is very helpful once the intersection of the two animals has occurred.
- The ultimate goal is to pass the animals all the way around the circle so both animals come back to you. However, it's better to move on to the next activity at the height of the laughter and energy even if the group has reached this goal.

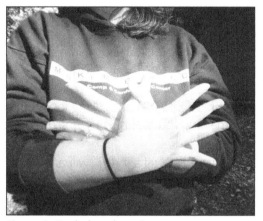

Figure A. Eagle hand motion

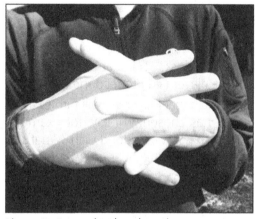

Figure B. Porcupine hand motion

Figure C. Passing the eagle

Figure D. Passing the porcupine

#48: Wanna Buy a Duck?

Objective: To have everyone "buy" an animal by the end of the game
Recommended Ages: 6 and up
Number of Players: 5 to 30
Energy Level: 2 AMPS
Formation: Sitting in a circle

Description:

- Ask each player to think about one animal and one thing that it does.
- Turn to the person on your right (#1) and say, "Hey, mister (or ma'am), wanna buy a duck?" Tell that player to respond with "What's it do?" Say, "It quacks." Tell the player (#1) to respond with "I'll take it!"
- Explain that Player #1 will turn to the person on his right (#2) and, using the animal he has chosen, will say, for example, "Hey, ma'am, you wanna buy a skunk?" to which #2 will respond with "What's it do?"
- Tell players that everyone who has already answered "What's it do?" will answer all the way back to the leader before Player #2 can say "I'll take it!"
- Give this as an example scenario:

  #1: "Hey, mister, wanna buy a skunk?"

  #2: "What's it do?"

  #1: "It smells." Then, each previous player adds his answer: "It barks," "It squeals," "It bites," etc.
- Explain that then #2 answers "I'll take it" and turns to the next player and asks, "Wanna buy … ?"

#49: What's Your Sign?

Objective: To get to know other players and be the last person sitting
Recommended Ages: 7 and up
Number of Players: 6 to 30
Energy Level: 5 AMPS
Formation: Sitting in a circle

Description:

- Ask players to think about their own personalities and to decide on a sign or motion that describes an aspect of their personality. For example, a person who likes to swim could mime swimming or a drummer could play drums or a basketball player could shoot imaginary balls.
- Invite the players to share their signs with the group.
- To begin the game, make your own sign and then someone else's sign. That player will do his sign and the sign of another player. Continue this manner of passing signs around the circle.
- If someone doesn't see and repeat his sign when another player makes it, that player has to stand. Tell players that the game ends when only one player is left sitting. Congratulate the "winner" with much pomp and silliness.

#50: Zip-Zap-Pop

Objective: To confuse other players while staying alert yourself
Recommended Ages: All
Number of Players: 6 or more
Energy Level: 3 AMPS
Formation: Sitting in a circle

Description:

- Teach the three basic moves of the game and the sound words that go with them:
    - ✓ Zip (Figure A): The player says "zip" and then places his right hand on top of his head, pointing to the person on his left.
    - ✓ Zap (Figure B): The player says "zap" and then places his hand under his chin, pointing to the player on his right.
    - ✓ Pop (Figure C): The player says "pop" and then claps both hands together with his fingers pointed at a player across the circle.
- Begin by saying "zip" and then pointing to the player on your left or "zap" and then pointing to the player on your right. Explain that that player pointed to can choose to say "zip," "zap," or "pop," accompanied by the corresponding motion.
- Encourage players to send the sounds and motions around or across the circle. Tell the group that when a player fails to make a movement on his turn or the motion doesn't match what he's said, he's "caught."

Leadership Tips:

- The easiest way to teach the game is to first send "zip" all the way around the circle and then send "zap" around the circle in the opposite direction. Add "pop" to keep the group on its toes.
- Normally, this game is played as an elimination game. You can add a fun twist by encouraging the eliminated players to "heckle" the remaining players by making silly faces or funny sounds in order to disrupt their concentration.
- Another alternative is to have players collect letters when they goof up. Select a short word, such as "zip." The first time someone messes up, they get a "z," the next time an "i," and finally a "p." Play until someone has collected all three letters.
- This game can be played just for fun, with no one being eliminated.

Figure A. Zip

Figure B. Zap

Figure C. Pop

#51: Zoom and Mooz

Objective: To pass a word or names around the circle as quickly as possible
Recommended Ages: All
Number of Players: 5 or more
Energy Level: 3 AMPS
Formation: Sitting or standing in a circle

Description:

- Explain that the word "zoom" will be said by everyone in the circle as quickly as possible.
- Begin by saying "zoom" to the person on your right, and have each player repeat the word to the person on his right until that word comes back to you.
- To add fun, you can send the word backward ("mooz") around the circle.
- For an additional challenge, simultaneously send "zoom" one way and "mooz" the other way.

Leadership Tips:

- You can have the players lie on their stomachs or backs, with their heads toward the center of the circle.
- You can have players speak, whisper, or shout the words "zoom" and "mooz."
- You can play this as a name game by having players say their own name to the person to the right. To send their names around backward, invite them to figure out how to say their names backward. For example: Jane becomes "enaj," Chris becomes "sirk," and Bob is "bob."
- Use this game as a teambuilding exercise by seeing how fast they can send a word around the circle. You will need a watch with a seconds feature or a volunteer to count seconds. Encourage them to keep working toward a faster time. Talk together afterward about what the group did to increase the time.

6

Mind Games

#52: Bang-Bang-Bang

Objective: To figure out who the leader "shoots"
Recommended Ages: 8 and up
Number of Players: 3 or more
Energy Level: 1 AMPS
Formation: Any in which the participants can hear each other

Description:

- Introduce this as a classic "mind" game. Tell the players they'll need to listen carefully in order to figure out the answer to your question.
- Explain that you'll say to the group, "Bang-bang-bang, who did I shoot?" and the goal is to figure out who was "shot." (The first player who makes any kind of a vocal sound, such as speaking or laughing, is the one who is shot.)
- Continue to ask the question until players figure out the answer.

Leadership Tips:

- A neat feature of this game is that you do not need to make plans in advance with a helper.
- Make sure everyone figures out the solution before moving on. Instead of telling the solution, it's always best to give hints to help people figure it out on their own.

#53: Bugs

Objective: To figure out how many imaginary bugs the leader has
Recommended Ages: 8 and up
Number of Players: 3 or more
Energy Level: 1 AMPS
Formation: Any in which the participants can hear each other

Description:

- Hold out your palm to the group and say, "How many bugs are in my hand?" Tell the players that the bugs are imaginary. Answers will vary.
- Let the players guess and either wait until someone guesses "7" or tell them the answer.
- Rephrase the question, asking, "How many bugs?" (The answer this time is "3.")
- Ask, "How many in there?" (The answer is "4.") Or ask, "How many bugs would you say are in my hand?" (The answer is "10.")
- Encourage players to figure out why the answer changes. (The answer depends on how many words are in the question.)

#54: Cash Only Store

Objective: To figure out what can be bought at the Cash Only Store—a real challenge!
Recommended Ages: 8 and up
Number of Players: 2 or more
Energy Level: 2 AMPS
Formation: Any in which the participants can hear each other

Description:

- Tell the group you're opening a Cash Only Store and that there are certain items they can buy and certain items they can't buy. Explain that it's their job to guess the items they can buy. Give these examples of items that they can purchase: cats, trees, balls, bats, lamps, cars, pens, maps, and tea. Then, give examples of items that they can't purchase: figs, knives, kites, gloves, coats, shoes, computers, rugs, bugs, or hugs.
- If participants get stuck, you can tell them as a hint that the Cash Only Store does not accept checks, credit cards, or IOUs. (Items that contain the vowels I, O, or U can't be purchased.)

Leadership Tips:

- To help participants, keep repeating "Sorry, no IOUs."
- Because this puzzle is more challenging than most, it's recommended you play several other mind games before this one so players will get some ideas about how to solve it.

#55: Costume Party

Objective: To figure out which characters are invited to the costume party
Recommended Ages: 8 and up
Number of Players: 3 to 30
Energy Level: 1 AMPS
Formation: Any in which the participants can hear each other

Description:

- Tell the players that they're invited to a pretend costume party, to which everyone should come dressed as a real or fictional character once they identify the character correctly. Let the group know that you're coming as someone such as Snoopy, Madonna, or Lincoln.
- Ask the players to decide which character they'd like to be and to announce their selection. (What you know and the players need to figure out is that the only people invited to the party are identified as one name. For example, if someone says he would like to come as Lincoln, he can come. However, if he wants to come as Abraham Lincoln, tell him that you're sorry and that he needs to choose another character.)

Leadership Tips:

- Have plenty of names ready as examples so everyone in the group will catch on, feel good about themselves, and be invited to the party. Some examples include: Milton, Homer, Gershwin, Wolverine, Caesar, Batman, or Godzilla.
- Typically, these single-word characters come in four different types. Many famous people are frequently identified by just their last name, such as: Columbus, Eisenhower, Churchill, Patton, etc. Some are well known by just their first name: Linus, Bugs, Daffy, Taz, Groucho, etc. Other real and fictional characters only have or use one name: Noah, Moses, Pocahontas, Socrates, Cher, Dumbo, Yoda, Shrek, etc. Lastly, some are well known by just a nickname, such as: Superman, Bones, Hawkeye, Rocky, etc.

#56: Draw the Man

Objective: To figure out the "right" way to draw a stick figure
Recommended Ages: 6 and up
Number of Players: 3 to 30
Energy Level: 2 AMPS
Formation: Any in which the participants can hear each other and see the leader

Description:

- Using just an index finger, draw a simple stick figure in the air, on the floor, on a wall, or wherever. The simpler the stick figure the better.
- Ask individuals to do exactly what they saw you do. Continue to do this until they get it right—which many may not be able to do. (The secret is that you use your left hand each time.)

#57: Fantastic Fruits (Big Fruits/Little Fruits)

Objective: To figure out which fruit has been chosen and why

Recommended Ages: 8 and up

Number of Players: 4 or more

Energy Level: 1 AMPS

Formation: Any in which the participants can hear each other. The leader needs a volunteer who knows the solution before the game begins.

Description:

- In advance, take a player aside and explain the game. Tell him that he should say "No" to all fruits you name until you name a small fruit, such as cherries, grapes, or strawberries. Explain that the fruit you name after the small fruit is one chosen by the group and to say "Yes" to that fruit. For example, if the fruit chosen by the group is "apples," the exchange may go like this:

    Leader: Is it oranges?

    Volunteer: No.

    Leader: Is it bananas?

    Volunteer: No.

    Leader: Is it blueberries?

    Volunteer: No.

    Leader: Is it apples?

    Volunteer: Yes!

- To begin the game, ask the volunteer to move out of hearing distance. When he's gone, have one of the players name a kind of fruit.
- When the volunteer returns, say the names of several different fruits, as noted previously. As if by magic or extrasensory perception, the volunteer will know the fruit that was chosen.
- Play several times until the players in the group figure out how the volunteer guesses right.

Leadership Tips:

- This is a difficult challenge. Be prepared to give such hints as "Is it a *gigantic* watermelon?" or "Is it a *tiny* raisin?"
- It's always best to let individuals figure out these games for themselves. Because letting players blurt out solutions can steal the joy of the "ah ha" moment for others, ask the player who thinks he knows the solution to go with the volunteer to check out his guess. In this way, players can figure out when they're on the right track without spoiling it for others.

#58: I Like Apples

Objective: To figure out the pattern of likes and dislikes
Recommended Ages: 8 and up
Number of Players: 3 or more
Energy Level: 1 AMPS
Formation: Any in which the participants can hear

Description:

- Explain that in this mental teaser, players will take turns telling the group one item they like and one item they dislike. Tell players that the statements don't have to be true but do have to follow a pattern. Tell them it's their job to figure out the pattern. (As the leader, you know that everyone likes things that contain double letters and dislikes items that don't have double letters.)
- Give them the following examples and then invite them to make their own statements:
    - ✓ I like cheese, but I don't like chairs.
    - ✓ I like floors, but I don't like corn.
    - ✓ I like Hawaii, but I don't like Georgia.
- Remind the players not to tell the answer if they figure out the key, but keep giving answers on their turns to help others recognize the pattern.

Leadership Tips:

- Be ready to respond in the following manner:
  Player: I like books, but I don't like doors.
  Leader: I'm sorry, but we like both of those.
  Player: I like ducks, but I don't like moose.
  Leader: Actually, we like moose, but we don't like ducks.
- It's helpful to have some items to mention that will help players see the pattern.
- Another helpful hint is that everybody is going to like and dislike the same things.
- Some good words to "like" are: Mississippi, pepperoni pizza, green apples, bookkeeping, etc.

#59: Number Magic

Objective: To figure out the pattern that signals the chosen number
Recommended Ages: 8 and up
Number of Players: 3 or more
Energy Level: 1 AMPS
Formation: Any in which the participants can hear. This game requires the leader to confer with a volunteer in advance.

Description:

- Prior to the beginning of the game, choose a volunteer to help you. Explain the secret code to the volunteer. Tell him you will say, "Helper, everyone can do this if they try; please tell us the chosen number." Tell the volunteer that in that example, the answer is five. Or give the following example: "Helper, do your best; please tell us the chosen number." (The answer is four.) Explain that the volunteer ignores the word "helper" and listens for the first letter of the first word in the instructions. Each letter represents a letter: A is one, B is two, C is three, etc. Using the alphabet this way, a fast-thinking partner could do up to 10, 15, or even 26.
- At the beginning of the game, ask a player to choose a number between one and five without the volunteer hearing the number. Explain that your helper is able to know the answer through "extrasensory perception" or "divine mystical power." The framing story doesn't matter because the game is just for fun.
- Continue to play until players figure out the secret. Again, encourage players not to blurt out the answer but to check by moving out of earshot with the volunteer.

#60: Picnic

Objective: To figure out what each individual can take on a picnic
Recommended Ages: 8 and up
Number of Players: 3 to 30
Energy Level: 1 AMPS
Formation: Any in which the participants can hear each other

Description:

- Announce that you're going on a picnic and want to invite everyone along. However, explain that a player can come only if he brings a specific item.
- As leader, you know that each player must bring an item that begins with the same letter or sound as his first name. For example, Sarah could bring strawberries but not jelly. Joshua could bring jelly but not bread.
- Invite everyone in the group to take turns naming one item he might bring. Some players will catch on quickly, and when their turn comes, they'll be able to name an item beginning with the first letter of their name. Keep going around until everyone can name an item to bring to the picnic.

Leadership Tips:

- This is one of the easier mind games and is a good game to start with if the group is unfamiliar with this type of game.
- Sometimes, a review is enough to help people out, such as: "Mike over there is bringing milk, melons, and mice. What are you bringing, Ruth?"

#61: Twin Cities

Objective: To figure out the pattern that signals the selected city
Recommended Ages: 10 and up
Number of Players: 3 or more
Energy Level: 1 AMPS
Formation: Any in which the participants can hear each other

Description:

- Confer with a volunteer in advance. Explain to the volunteer that the city selected by the group will be the one listed *after* you say a city with a two-word name, such as Los Angeles. Give the following example, in which the city selected is Baltimore:
  Leader: Is it Cleveland?
  Volunteer: No.
  Leader: Is it Weeki Wachi?
  Volunteer: No.
  Leader: Is it Baltimore?
  Volunteer: Yes!
- Have the volunteer leave the area while someone selects the name of a city. When the volunteer returns, begin listing cities and follow the pattern.
- Play until everyone has figured out the solution.

Leadership Tips:

- You can give the helpful hint of exaggerating the two-word city—even pausing between the two words.
- As with all mind games, never tell the solution. Let those who think they know the solution leave with the volunteer and test their theories away from the group.

7

Drama Games

#62: Adverb

Objective: To guess the adverb the players are performing
Recommended Ages: 10 and up
Number of Players: 6 or more
Energy Level: 4 AMPS
Formation: Equal groups, with about five or six to a group and no fewer than three in a group

Description:

- Divide players into groups.
- Ask each group to choose an adverb without the other group hearing.
- Choose one group to start and to perform its adverb. The other groups try to guess what the adverb is. The team that guesses correctly first scores a point, although scorekeeping isn't important.
- Warn the players that the only action they can perform is the adverb itself.

Leadership Tips:

- Remind your groups that most words ending in "ly" are adverbs, such as: slowly, quickly, fluidly, softly, angrily, hungrily, majestically, etc.
- This is a good activity to use when you want to discuss communication. Invite players to notice that body language is integral to communication. Discuss how their bodies reflect what they're saying. Encourage them to think about what happens when their body language is communicating something very different than their words.

#63: B-Movie Voice-Over Theater

Objective: To improvise a scene as "led" by two offstage participants

Recommended Ages: 10 and up

Number of Players: 10 or more

Energy Level: 5 AMPS

Formation: Standing in two lines, with each assigned to one side of the "stage" or play area

Description:

- Explain that this is an improvisational game based on foreign movies that are frequently poorly dubbed, so the words and the actor's mouths never match.
- Tell players that to begin, two actors will be onstage acting out an improvised scene. Off to stage right and stage left, two other actors are saying the lines and determining what the actors on stage are doing.
- Be sure that the two actors on stage know they're to interact as the offstage voices lead them.
- Tell players that as actors alternately leave the stage, the person doing the offstage voice becomes the new actor onstage.

Leadership Tips:

- It's important to know the maturity level of your group.
- This game is a lot of fun, but the group should understand that no one onstage can be put in a situation that might compromise self-esteem.

#64: Emotion Relay

Objective: To portray a wide range of emotions

Recommended Ages: 10 and up

Number of Players: 12 to 60

Energy Level: 9 AMPS

Formation: Standing in four equal teams placed in the four corners of the playing area to form a square or three teams placed as a triangle

Description:

- Have each of the four groups choose an Emotion Leader, who will sit cross-legged on the floor, facing the center of the play area. Have the rest of the team stand in a line behind their leader.
- Give the signal to "go" or "curtain," since it's a drama game.
- Have the first person in line run clockwise to the next team's Emotion Leader, sit directly in front of the Emotion Leader, and then count to 10. Explain that the Emotion Leader is to act out any emotion of his choosing.
- The runner is to follow the lead of the Emotion Leader's emotion while counting to 10. For example, if the Emotion Leader is crying, the runner cries while counting to 10; if the Emotion Leader is yelling from anger, the runner counts to 10 angrily.
- Encourage Emotion Leaders to use a wide variety of emotions.
- Tell runners that when they return to their own teams they will become the new Emotion Leaders for their teams. Explain that the previous Emotion Leader will move to the back of the line. The first person standing in line runs to the next station.

Leadership Tips:

- Even though this is a standard relay race, let all teams finish so everyone gets to participate.
- This makes a great a discussion starter about communication.

#65: Freeze

Objective: To learn or improve improvisational skills or simply to have fun
Recommended Ages: 10 and up
Number of Players: 6 or more
Energy Level: 6 AMPS
Formation: Standing or sitting in a circle

Description:

- Have two volunteers go to the center of the circle and begin to improvise a scene by using whatever characters or situations come to mind.
- Explain to players in the circle that they're to watch the two characters. If they see a great place to begin an entirely new scene, they're to yell "Freeze!" Tell everyone that at that point the two center characters are to freeze in place.
- The player who yelled "Freeze!" is to go into the circle and tap one of the two frozen actors on the shoulder. The new player will compliment that person for doing a good job, and the tapped player will join the circle.
- Explain that the new player now has to begin a scene with the remaining frozen actor who comes back to life as soon as the new actor starts their scene.

Leadership Tip:

- Point out that no one should have any shame in being asked to leave the circle. Be sure everyone understands that actors are selecting a pose or word to interact with and not a person or personality.

#66: Hitchhiker

Objective: To improvise a scene in which three players catch the affliction of the fourth
Recommended Ages: 10 and up
Number of Players: 8 or more
Energy Level: 6 AMPS
Formation: Standing

Description:

- Show the group four imaginary spaces in a car. Have the group form a line. Assign the first four players a seat in the car. Place one in the driver's seat and two in the backseat Ask the fourth one to play a hitchhiker trying to get a lift on the side of the road.
- Have that the driver "stop" the car and invite the hitchhiker to get in. The four actors in the car will "drive" down the road.
- Explain that subtly at first, the hitchhiker will begin to exhibit some affliction through movement that's contagious to the others in the car.
- Once everyone in the car has caught the affliction, yell "Switch!" Tell everyone to rotate positions in the car so the next person in line becomes the new hitchhiker. A typical rotation would be:
  ✓ The hitchhiker moves to the driver's seat.
  ✓ The driver moves to the backseat on the right behind the hitchhiker.
  ✓ The player behind the hitchhiker moves to behind the driver.
  ✓ The player behind the driver gets out of the car and returns to the line.

Leadership Tips:

- The possibilities for afflictions are endless, such as: coughing, sneezing, itching, sleeping, twitching, paranoia, hiccups, etc.
- Give everyone a turn so the original driver becomes the last one to be the hitchhiker.
- Keep the action moving. Be sure the next person in line is ready to go!

#67: Please/No

Objective: To get the volunteer to "break character"
Recommended Ages: 6 and up
Number of Players: 4 or more
Energy Level: 3 AMPS
Formation: Standing in a circle, with a player in the center

Description:

- Ask one player to get in the center or "onstage" and then mime a scene or emotion.
- Tell the other players to go up to this player one by one and try to get him to smile, laugh, or break character somehow.
- Explain that the player trying to get the center player to break character can only use the word *please* and the player in the center can only use the word *no*.
- Whoever "breaks" the person in the center takes his place, and the play continues.

Leadership Tips:

- Remind players that only the two words are allowed and that touching is ruled out.
- This is a terrific game for teaching young drama students the importance of not laughing, giggling, or snickering onstage. They can learn to simply resist showing themselves instead of the character they're playing. This game gives players an opportunity to develop a little more confidence in not "breaking" character.

#68: Smile Gauntlet

Objective: To make the volunteer laugh or smile
Recommended Ages: 10 and up
Number of Players: 10 to 40
Energy Level: 4 AMPS
Formation: Standing in two equal lines, facing each other

Description:

- One by one, have the players walk between the lines from one end to the other, looking each player in the eyes as he passes.
- Explain that it's the goal of the other players to make the player walking between the lines laugh or smile.
- Do not allow any touching.

Leadership Tips:

- Encourage everyone present to try the "gauntlet." Be sure everyone understands that the gauntlet—the challenge—is a choice.
- As a drama game, this teaches the importance of staying "in character" and not smiling at inappropriate times.
- This also works as a circle game. The player in the center tries to make the players in the circle laugh or smile. When that player succeeds, he trades places with the player who smiled or laughed.

#69: Train Station/Bus Stop

Objective: Two participants improvise a first-time meeting
Recommended Ages: 10 and up
Number of Players: 6 or more
Energy Level: 5 AMPS
Formation: Sitting in a horseshoe

Description:

- To begin, designate one end of the horseshoe as the beginning of the line. Identify the open area in front of players as the "stage"—the waiting area for a bus or a train.
- Have one player wait "onstage" for their transportation to arrive. Explain that the person at the head of the line will join the player already waiting and will begin the scene. Tell players that the first "waiting" player is to react to the other incoming player, and when the time is right for the scene to end, the waiting player is to get on his bus or train.
- Explain that the second player now becomes the waiting actor and the next person in line enters the "stage."
- This game gives each player the chance to perform two scenes with two different people.

Leadership Tips:

- This game can also be played as a friendly competition to see which of the two actors "breaks" character first by smiling, laughing, smirking, etc. The actor who breaks character leaves the stage and the other player remains until someone else "breaks" character. Occasionally, you may wish to send in a challenger if a scene starts to drag.
- You can choose someone to be "first in line" who will be a good example of acting and who doesn't fear improvisation.

#70: Whopper

Objective: To guess which of the volunteer's three autobiographical stories isn't true
Recommended Ages: 10 and up
Number of Players: 2 to 30
Energy Level: 2 AMPS
Formation: Sitting in a circle

Description:

- Explain that part of being a good actor is the ability to lie. Point out that acting is one of the few occasions where not telling the truth well is an asset.
- Tell players that the goal of the players in this activity is to convince others that he's another person.
- Invite the players to think of two stories or incidents that actually happened to them and make up a third story of something that didn't happen.
- Tell the group that once a player tells his three tales, the rest of the group is to guess by voting which was true and which was the lie.

Leadership Tip:

- This is also a good "get acquainted" activity.

#71: Wipe That Smile Off Your Face

Objective: To follow the commands to smile or not smile
Recommended Ages: 10 and up
Number of Players: 6 to 50
Energy Level: 3 AMPS
Formation: Sitting in a circle

Description:

- Select a volunteer to stand in the center of the circle. Explain to the other players that the volunteer wants their seat and can have it only if they refuse to follow the volunteer's commands. Tell them that the volunteer can only give three commands:
    - ✓ "Smile please!" (The player in the circle smiles. The person receiving the command should also smile.)
    - ✓ "Wipe that smile off your face!" (The player in the circle makes a wiping motion with his hand, and changes a smile to a frown.)
    - ✓ "Throw that smile to somebody else." (The player in the circle should pantomime grabbing the smile off his face and throwing it to another player in the circle, who should begin smiling.)
- Have the volunteer give anyone in the circle the commands.
- If any of the three commands isn't followed, the person who failed to follow the given direction replaces the volunteer in the center.

Leadership Tips:

- Some games such as #67: Please/No and #68: Smile Gauntlet are terrific for teaching the basics of not breaking character. This game takes those games one step further.
- In larger groups, have the player "throwing a smile" call the name of the player to whom he's sending the smile.

8

Group Builders

#72: Clap On, Clap Off!

Objective: To guide the volunteer by using only the sound of clapping hands
Recommended Ages: 10 and up
Number of Players: 5 or more
Energy Level: 6 AMPS
Formation: Sitting

Description:

- Send a volunteer away from the group temporarily.
- Ask the group to decide what task is to be performed, such as touching a particular object, doing jumping jacks, singing, hugging a particular individual, etc.
- Call the volunteer back to the group, and as he approaches, the group begins to clap—clapping more vigorously as the volunteer gets closer to achieving the goal and clapping less when the volunteer gets off track. When the goal is accomplished, the group breaks into wild applause and cheering.
- Instruct the successful volunteer to choose a new volunteer, who leaves the group while a new goal is chosen, and the game begins again.

Leadership Tips:

- It's best to start with something simple, such as touching an object, such as a player's wristwatch or shoe.
- As the game progresses, the tasks can become more sophisticated.
- While this is a great game just for fun, it makes a good discussion for the role of praise and encouragement in relationships. Ask questions, such as: How do you feel when you are encouraged? How do you feel when you're given no praise or feedback? How can this group be more encouraging?

#73: Freeway Follies

Objective: To explore communication in a noisy environment (a blind activity)
Recommended Ages: 12 and up
Number of Players: 8 to 30
Energy Level: 7 AMPS
Formation: Standing in pairs, with one person behind the other

Description:

- Explain to the pairs that the person in front is the car and the one in back is the driver. Have the front player (the car) close his eyes.
- Tell the driver to place his hands on the shoulders of the car and guide the car through "traffic." Tell the car to hold his hands in front, with the palms out as bumpers. Encourage the players who are driving to make such car noises as honking, racing engines, and squealing brakes, although they can't speak.
- Give drivers clear boundaries. Suggest they vary speed safely throughout the activity.
- Demonstrate with a volunteer, but don't give any hints about how the partners can communicate nonverbally.
- After a few minutes, signal for the participants to switch roles.

Leadership Tips:

- Be aware that some people are very uncomfortable being "blind" or having to shut their eyes. You can offer blindfolds as an alternative as well as the opportunity to opt out once you've described the game.
- If you do this activity along with other blind activities, it's best to debrief all of them together.
- Use the following questions to debrief the activity:
    - ✓ Did you prefer being the car or the driver? Why?
    - ✓ How does it feel to be guided by touch?
    - ✓ Did the noises make it easier or more difficult?
    - ✓ What did you learn about yourself?

#74: Hike in the Dark

Objective: To explore communication by guiding and being guided by spoken cues only (a blind activity)
Recommended Ages: 12 and up
Number of Players: 4 to 30
Energy Level: 5 AMPS
Formation: Standing in pairs

Description:

- Explain that one partner will close his eyes while the other sighted partner takes the blind person on a hike.
- As with other blind activities, reassure players that they can choose to opt out or use a blindfold instead closing their eyes.
- Tell them that their partners can't touch or connect physically in any way. The sighted person can only give spoken cues, such as "Take three steps forward," "Turn right," etc.
- After a few minutes, signal for the participants to switch roles.

Leadership Tips:

- If you do this activity along with other blind activities, it's best to debrief all of them together.
- Use the following questions to debrief the activity:
    ✓ Did you prefer being sighted or blind? Why?
    ✓ How did it feel to be guided by words?
    ✓ What did you like about your partner's communication?
    ✓ What was frustrating? What was funny?
    ✓ What did you learn about yourself?

#75: Imagination Toss

Objective: To toss and catch a variety of imaginary objects while learning names
Recommended Ages: 10 and up
Number of Players: 8 to 20
Energy Level: 6 AMPS
Formation: Standing in a circle

Description:

- Instruct the players to place their hands on their heads.
- Call out the name of someone across the circle and then toss an imaginary tennis ball to that person.
- Explain that the recipient is to bring his hands down and pretend to catch the ball. Encourage that player to use as much drama as he wishes. Tell the recipient to call out the name of someone else across the circle and then toss the imaginary ball. Tell players to remember the player who threw them the ball and to whom they threw the ball.
- Tell players to leave their hands down once they've "caught" the ball. Tell the last player to toss it back to you.
- Explain that in the second round that the group will be throwing a "watermelon." Tell them to use the same pattern as the first round.
- In subsequent rounds, toss objects of different sizes, such as a Ping-Pong® ball and/or an egg.

Leadership Tips:

- Once the group is familiar with the pattern, have them try tossing the object in reverse order.
- For a group that enjoys being challenged, have them simultaneously toss an object in the original direction and another object in the reverse direction.
- If the group has been learning names, at the end of the activity, invite player to see if someone can identify everyone in the group.
- This can also be used as a drama game.
- Use the following questions to debrief the activity:
  ✓ How was the group successful?
  ✓ How did you feel tossing something you couldn't see?
  ✓ If someone intentionally broke the object, how did you feel?
  ✓ If you were on the receiving end of a broken or wildly thrown object, how did you respond?
  ✓ How would this game be different if real objects were used?
  ✓ What did you learn about the group?

#76: Photographer

Objective: To explore communication by guiding and being guided silently by touch (a blind and silent activity)

Recommended Ages: 10 and up

Number of Players: 8 to 30

Energy Level: 3 AMPS

Formation: Standing in pairs, with one behind the other

Description:

- Explain that the person in front is the camera and the one behind is the photographer. Tell players that neither photographers nor cameras can speak.
- Tell the photographer to gently place his hands on the shoulders of the camera and silently guide the camera to the object, person, or scenery he wishes to photograph. Explain that photographers can "set up" the picture by positioning the camera (moving the head gently to an angle or having the camera sit or kneel).
- Tell players that in order to take a picture, the photographer will gently touch the ear of the camera. The camera will respond by quickly opening and closing his eyes like the shutter of a real camera.
- Demonstrate the photographer's role with a volunteer camera. Have players switch roles after they've taken three to five photos.

Leadership Tips:

- You can make the exercise more challenging by having players take at least five pictures and asking the camera if he remembers all the snapshots—perhaps even returning to where they were taken.
- As with other blind activities, reassure players that they can choose to opt out or use a blindfold instead closing their eyes.
- An alternate approach to "operating the shutter" on the camera would be to tap the shoulder of the camera twice. Some may find touching the ear too personal.
- If this activity is used with other blind activities, it's best to debrief all of them together.
- Use the following questions to debrief the activity:
    - ✓ Did you prefer being the photographer or the camera? For what reasons?
    - ✓ How does it feel to be guided by touch?
    - ✓ Did silence make it easier or more difficult?
    - ✓ What did you learn about yourself?

#77: Suey, Suey

Objective: To explore communication by guiding another by intonation only (a blind activity)
Recommended Ages: 12 and up
Number of Players: 4 to 30
Energy Level: 5 AMPS
Formation: Standing in pairs

Description:

- Tell one partner to close his eyes. Explain that the sighted person will lead the blind one by repeating the word *suey* as if calling a pig.
- Tell the partners that they're not allowed to touch or connect physically in any way. Explain that the sighted person will use the intonation of his voice to indication direction, distance, or danger.
- Demonstrate how this is done, especially including an intonation to indicate "stop."
- After a few minutes, signal for the participants to switch roles.

Leadership Tips:

- If you use this activity with other blind activities, it's best to debrief all of them together.
- As with other blind activities, reassure players that they can choose to opt out or use a blindfold instead closing their eyes.
- Use the following questions to debrief the activity:
    ✓ Did you prefer being sighted or blind? Why?
    ✓ How does it feel to be guided by sound?
    ✓ What did you like about your partner's communication?
    ✓ What was frustrating? What was funny?
    ✓ What did you learn about yourself?
- #74: Hike in the Dark, #76: Photographer, and this game work well together to have a discussion of three of the most important ways we communicate: physical touch, verbal direction, and intonation. Ask players which form of communication they prefer. Invite them to reflect on what happens when a leader communicates differently than the preferred method of the listener.
- You can use this activity as an introduction to a Bible study about the Good Shepherd. Read John 10:1-18 and then ask:
    ✓ How easy or difficult was it to distinguish your partner's voice from those around you?
    ✓ What are the other voices that distract us today?
    ✓ What do we need to do to focus on the Good Shepherd's voice?

#78: Timeline

Objective: To explore silent communication while learning more about each other
Recommended Ages: 10 and up
Number of Players: 8 or more
Energy Level: 3 AMPS
Formation: Standing in a straight line

Description:

- Ask participants to line up in a straight line by the month and day of their birth without speaking.
- Point toward the end of the line that represents January and the one that represents December.
- Explain that anyone born January 1 is the beginning of the line and anyone born December 31 is the end of the line.
- Once they think they're in order, ask them to say their birthdays out loud.

Leadership Tips:

- This is an excellent way to begin a discussion on how we communicate with each other.
- You can also have people line up silently by age or alphabetically by middle name.

#79: Spot

Objective: To build trust and to teach good spotting technique—an essential safety skill for players to have before engaging in any activity that involves lifting, falling, or other physical risks
Recommended Ages: 12 and up
Number of Players: 4 to 30
Energy Level: 6 AMPS
Formation: Standing in pairs with someone of similar size and weight

Description:

- Have one partner stand behind the other, facing the same direction about one foot apart. Players need to be of similar weight. Have players switch places if partners have a difference of more than 50 pounds in body weight or six inches in height.
- Have partners decide who will spot first and who will be the "faller."

- Have the fallers stand straight, with their arms crossed across their chests and their hands flat on their shoulders. Tell them they can fall with their eyes opened or closed.
- Have the spotters stand directly behind the faller, facing the same direction.
- Instruct the spotters to stand with one foot ahead of the other, their knees slightly bent, and their hands held up, with their palms out about shoulder height.
- Explain that each pair must speak the following dialogue before the faller falls:
  Faller: Ready?
  Spotter: Ready!
  Faller: Falling.
  Spotter: Fall on.
- Tell pairs that when they have completed this conversation that the faller falls backward toward the spotter, keeping his body very stiff and bending only at the ankles. Explain that the spotter must catch his partner and gently push him back into a standing position.
- Explain that the faller will take a small step forward and then repeat the dialogue and the fall. Tell the pairs they can continue with the faller stepping out a little farther each time. Be sure they understand they should switch roles at the point when either feels uncomfortable with continuing.
- Demonstrate the activity with a volunteer before any of the pairs begin. Explain that the goal of spotting is simply to break someone's fall, keeping his head and back protected. Tell them that if someone's buttocks hit the ground, they should not consider it a failure.
- Explain that all players must adhere to the following rules or they'll be asked to sit out the activity:
  ✓ No one is to fall until the conversation is completed and the partner is ready.
  ✓ No one is to bend at the waist or sit because this will guarantee that the spotter won't be able to catch the faller.

Leadership Tips:

- Use the following questions to debrief the activity:
  ✓ Did you prefer being the spotter or the person falling? Why?
  ✓ What, if anything, about this activity made you uncomfortable?
  ✓ What did you like about the activity?
  ✓ Why was communication important?
  ✓ What did you learn about yourself?
- Do *not* hesitate to pull out a player if you feel uncomfortable about his serious desire to keep his partner safe.

#80: Go With the Flow

Objective: To build trust and practice good spotting techniques (use after teaching the spotting techniques described in #79: Spot)

Recommended Ages: 12 and up

Number of Players: Multiples of 9

Energy Level: 6 AMPS

Formation: Standing shoulder to shoulder in a circle, with a volunteer in the center

Description:

- Once players have demonstrated their ability to spot, have them stand together shoulder to shoulder, with a volunteer in the center. Be sure the volunteer knows what will happen in the activity.
- Have players in the circle take a spotting posture, and check that no gaps exist between them in the circle. Have stronger players distribute themselves evenly around the circle.
- Explain that they'll repeat the following pattern before the volunteer falls:

  Volunteer in the center: Ready?

  Circle: Ready!

  Volunteer in the center: Falling.

  Circle: Fall on.
- Explain that when this pattern is completed to the satisfaction of everyone, the volunteer will fall backward or forward toward the circle, keeping his body very stiff, crossing his arms across his chest, and bending only at the ankles.
- Explain that the players in the circle will gently catch and pass the volunteer back and forth across the circle. When done correctly, it will be like a massage for the person in the center.
- After a minute or so, have a new volunteer take the place in the center.
- Demonstrate the activity by being the first volunteer.
- Repeat the cautions:
  - ✓ Volunteers should fall only if the conversation has been completed and the circle is ready.
  - ✓ Volunteers shouldn't bend at the waist or sit. Otherwise, the members of the circle won't be able to catch them.

Leadership Tips:

- Pay very close attention to the maturity exhibited by the group. Don't allow participants to be silly or "bounce" the center person back and forth.
- Stop the activity if at any point you feel uncomfortable about a person's ability to keep someone else safe.

- If someone does fall, it's important for the group to talk about what happened before deciding whether to continue the activity.
- Use the following questions to debrief the activity:
  - ✓ Did you prefer being in the circle or the one falling? Why?
  - ✓ What part of this activity made you uncomfortable?
  - ✓ What did you like about the activity?
  - ✓ Why was communication important?
  - ✓ What did you learn about yourself?

#81: Parting of the Sea

Objective: To build trust among a mature group that knows each other
Recommended Ages: 12 and up
Number of Players: 4 to 30
Energy Level: 6 AMPS
Formation: Standing in two lines, facing each other, about four feet apart

Description:

- The group stands in two equal lines, facing each other, with an opening between them. Have them decide which end is the entrance.
- Have each player raise the arm that is farthest from the entrance toward the line of players facing them at shoulder height. Tell them that the resulting pattern should look like a zipper.
- Have a volunteer stand about 10 feet from the entrance to the lines and begin the following pattern:

  Volunteer: Ready?

  Lines: Ready!

  Volunteer: Walking.

  Lines: Walk on.
- Tell the volunteer to walk into the path between the lines with his eyes open. Explain to the players in the lines that their goal is for each player to lift his arm to vertical just before the volunteer gets to his arm without touching the volunteer. This will create the illusion of a wave parting just ahead.
- Once the volunteer crosses the path completely, have him select a new volunteer and then take the volunteer's place in the line.
- If the group enjoys this challenge and handled it responsibly, you can take it to the next level by having the volunteers run. Be sure everyone understands that if the group fails to keep volunteers safe, you'll stop the activity immediately and debrief it.

Leadership Tips:

- Know your group. This game is safest with groups with a high sense of individual responsibility.
- It's a good idea to evaluate the group's ability to be successful and trustworthy by demonstrating this activity as the first volunteer.
- Discourage the volunteer moving between the line from wearing a cap with a bill or brim. This can become a target that can distract from the point of the activity.
- Use the following questions to debrief the activity:
    - ✓ Did you prefer being the volunteer or part of the sea? Why?
    - ✓ If you volunteered to walk through, what motivated you?
    - ✓ What about this activity made you uncomfortable?
    - ✓ What did you like about the activity?
    - ✓ What did you learn about yourself?
    - ✓ What did you learn about the group?
- You can use this activity to lead into a discussion about Moses and the Israelites escaping from Egypt.

9

High Energy

#82: Wolf in Sheep's Clothing

Objective: To steal "sheep" from the other team

Recommended Ages: 10 and up

Number of Players: 20 to 60

Energy Level: 10 AMPS for the wolf and 2 AMPS for the sheep

Formation: Divide the group into two equal teams, with each sitting at opposite ends of the playing area

Description:

- Explain to the groups that they are flocks of sheep. Have them practice saying "Baa! Baa!"
- Tell each team to select one fast runner to be the wolf. Have the two wolves meet with you in the center of the area.
- Explain that when you give the signal, they should run as fast as they can to the other flock and tap as many of the sheep on the head as they can. Explain that they have the time it takes you to sing the first verse of "Mary Had a Little Lamb" to tap their sheep.
- At the end of the song, ask the two wolves to say how many sheep they each tapped. If Wolf A tapped 10 sheep and Wolf B tapped 12 sheep, Wolf B is allowed to pick any two sheep from Wolf A's team.
- Once the sheep have switched flocks, have the groups choose two other wolves for the next round.
- Continue play for five rounds or until one wolf taps everyone on a side.

Leadership Tips:

- For larger groups, sing two verses of "Mary Had A Little Lamb." Vary the tempo to add an element of surprise.
- A wolf may only run once for each team, no matter how many times the player may switch teams.
- Encourage the flocks to continue to say "Baa! Baa!" loudly as the wolf runs among them. Younger children can get on all fours and try to run away from the wolf.

#83: Barnyard Hens

Objective: To mix up players into new groups of friends
Recommended Ages: 8 and up
Number of Players: 20 to 200
Energy Level: 9 AMPS
Formation: Scatter in groups of three around the playing area

Description:

- Tell each set of three to line up and then put their hands on the hips of the person in front of them.
- For every two groups, select one person to freely roam the area.
- Explain that when you give the signal, the lone player is to try to attach to the rear of one of the sets of three. When this happens, the player in the front of the set (the hen) takes off and will try to find another set of three to join. Once joined to the new set, the hen in that set will leave to look for a new set to join.

Leadership Tips:

- If you use a large play area, set clear boundaries so the groups stay fairly close to each other.
- Remove all potential hazards before you begin.

#84: Everyone's "It" Tag

Objective: To be the last person standing
Recommended Ages: 8 and up
Number of Players: 10 to 100
Energy Level: 9 AMPS
Formation: Standing in an open playing area

Description:

- Define the area of play by using real or established boundaries. In this game, the size of the area doesn't matter much as long as everyone can move safely.
- Explain that unlike tag games in which one person who is "it" tries to get everyone else, in this game, everyone is "it."
- Tell the players that when you give the signal, they're to try to tag as many other players as possible.
- Explain that when players are tagged, they should drop to one knee and keep on tagging as others run by. Tell them that the goal of this game is to be the last person standing.

#85: Hook 'Em

Objective: To have fun playing tag
Recommended Ages: 8 and up
Number of Players: 7 to 100
Energy Level: 9 AMPS
Formation: Standing in pairs scattered over the playing area

Description:

- Choose two people—one to be the "chaser" and the other to be the "chasee"—and explain that these players will try to tag one another on your signal.
- Have the remaining partners link elbows and stay still.
- Explain that in this tag game, as the chasee becomes tired, he will link elbows on one side of one of the pairs. Tell them that the other partner will disconnect from the group, become the chasee, and begin to run.
- If a "chasee" is tagged by the "chaser," these players switch roles.
- When a lot of people are playing, you can have more than one set of chasers and chasees to involve more people.

Leadership Tips:

- Because some children just like to be chased, especially with young kids, tell them they have only until you count to 10 to link up with a pair and send someone else to be chased. This will involve more people.
- When you have more than one set of chasees/chasers, it helps to distinguish who's being chased. One suggestion is to have chasees run with one hand behind their backs, which encourages more linking. You can also have a chaser tag any available chasee, which adds to the general chaos and fun of this game.

#86: I'm Late, I'm Late, I'm Late …

Objective: To return to an empty spot and rejoin the circle
Recommended Ages: 7 and up
Number of Players: 12 to 60
Energy Level: 8 AMPS
Formation: Standing in a circle, holding hands

Description:

- Explain that one player will roam around the outside of the circle and step in between two players standing in the circle. The player will gently separate their hands and say, "Run, bunnies."
- The two players will leave the circle and run around the outside in opposite directions. As they run around the circle, the player who stepped into the circle will take the hand of the person on either his right or left and join the circle, leaving only one space in the circle for one of the runners/bunnies.
- Explain that when the two running bunnies meet on the opposite side of the circle, they should shake their hands three times and say, "I'm late, I'm late, I'm late for a very important date—no time to say "Hello" (raise right hand), "Goodbye" (raise left hand). I'm late, I'm late, I'm late!" Then, they should shake hands three times again.
- Tell them that when they're finished, they should pass each other and continue running for the empty space in the circle. The first player back joins the circle and the second player becomes the roaming player who separates two new players to run and then rejoins the circle.

Leadership Tips:

- When you're playing with younger children, you may want to shorten the greeting to simply "I'm late, I'm late, I'm late" and then let them continue running.
- Because enthusiastic runners can easily collide, caution players to approach each other safely and to shake hands gently.

#87: Partners Tag

Objective: To tag your partner and then escape
Recommended Ages: 6 and up
Number of Players: 2 to 100
Energy Level: 9 AMPS
Formation: Standing in pairs

Description:

- Define the play area so players will know exactly where the boundaries are. Choose a small controlled space that keeps players reasonably and safely contained, such as a fellowship hall, half of a basketball court, a small yard, etc.
- Explain that in this tag game, their partner is the only person they will touch. Select one partner in each pair, such as the tallest, the one wearing blue, etc., to be the tagger and the other to be the "tagee."
- Tell players that on your signal, they should begin the chase. Point out that because the space is limited, speed may not be the best asset and that hiding may be a more useful skill.
- Explain that once a partner is tagged, there should be a delay time during which the tagged partner does a short activity before the new pursuit begins. Examples of short activities include spinning around three times, counting to 10, doing five jumping jacks, reciting the alphabet, or all of these in some combination.
- Be sure they understand that the tagged person must complete the short activity before pursuing his partner.

Leadership Tips:

- If your recreation time has a theme, such as Christmas party or a Fourth of July picnic, invent a delay that matches the theme, such as singing "Jingle Bells" or "Yankee Doodle."
- For creative groups, allow each set of partners to invent their own delay.
- If you want to step it up a notch, have the partner link elbows to make a team. Then, have two teams chase each other, following the same rules.

#88: Spinning Wool

Objective: To tag a designated player being protected by two other players
Recommended Ages: 8 and up
Number of Players: 4 to 100
Energy Level: 9 AMPS
Formation: Groupings of four

Description:

- When everyone's standing in a group of four, have them select one player to be a wolf who steps aside for the moment. Have the three other players—the sheep—form a triangle by joining hands/hooves.
- Explain that in this game, the goal of the three sheep is to band together and keep out the hungry wolf. Choose one sheep to be the wolf's intended victim.
- Tell the players that on your signal, the wolf will try to tag the selected sheep while the other two sheep try to keep the wolf away from him by spinning the group in a circle without dropping hands.
- Explain that if the wolf tags the selected sheep, the two exchange places and begin play again with their roles reversed. Once both players have had a chance to be a wolf and a sheep, allow the remaining two in the triangle their chance to play those roles.

Leadership Tips:

- With younger groups, it's easiest to simply count off "1, 2, 3, 4" so Player 1 is the wolf first, Player 2 is the sheep to be protected, etc.
- When many groups are playing at once, it's best to call time after 20 seconds or so and then let the sheep and wolf exchange roles. This ensures that everyone gets to do every job.

#89: Tentacle Tag

Objective: To tag the "minnows"
Recommended Ages: 6 and up
Number of Players: 10 to 100
Energy Level: 8 AMPS
Formation: Standing on the playing area

Description:

- Define the boundaries for this game. (You can use a tree or something you have with you to define the "riverbanks.")
- Ask a fairly fast player to volunteer to be the giant squid. Have all the other players—the minnows—line up on one end of the play area (the riverbank).
- Explain that when you yell "Swim!" the minnows should run/swim to the safety of the other side of the river without being tagged by the squid.
- Tell players that if they're tagged, they should kneel on one knee and begin to help the squid by tagging others as they run by. Once everyone who wasn't tagged safely makes it to the other side, yell "Swim!" again, sending the minnows back through the tentacles.
- Repeat the play until everyone has been tagged.

Leadership Tips:

- This game works best in a confined space with clear boundaries, such as a picnic shelter or a basketball court.
- It's recommended that you not play this game on asphalt surfaces.

#90: Walking Tag

Objective: To play a no-elimination tag game
Recommended Ages: 8 and up
Number of Players: 10 to 100
Energy Level: 8 AMPS
Formation: Standing in pairs

Description:

- Define the boundaries for this game. You'll need a space at least the size of half a basketball court and rectangular in shape.
- Designate one partner to be the chaser and one the "chasee."
- Explain that on your signal, the chaser will pursue the chasee but that they both can only walk.
- Tell the players that when a chasee is tagged that the partners will switch roles. The new chaser must spin around three times before giving pursuit.
- Once the players have mastered the basic walking tag, introduce a "moving wall." Gather one-half of the pairs. Have them link arms along one of the boundaries to form a wall, with you in the center.
- Continue to play the game as presented here, except that the players in the wall now move slowly forward so they shrink the size of the play area. Eventually, no play area will remain. When this happens, have the two groups switch places so those who were the wall become the chasers and chasees and the other group becomes the wall.

Leadership Tip:

- If the play area is undefined, divide the group of pairs into thirds. Have two-thirds of the players join hands to form a circle around the remaining players. The chase then takes place inside the circle. Slowly shrink the circle by moving toward the center. Play until each third of the players has had a turn at tag.

10

General Silliness

#91: Family Photo

Objective: To guess the unusual family posed by the other team
Recommended Ages: 12 and up
Number of Players: 6 to 30
Energy Level: 3 AMPS
Formation: Two equal teams standing and facing each other

Description:

- Have the two groups face each other and then choose a group to close its eyes. Encourage the group members to keep their eyes shut because it enhances the effect of this game.
- Ask the group with its eyes open to pose as an unusual family (see the list below for suggestions) to have a family portrait taken.
- Once the group is in position, ask the other group to look at the "photograph" and guess who the family is.
- Once everyone has enjoyed this fake photograph, have the groups switch roles so the other team has a turn to create a photograph.
- Feel free to add any creative families to the following list of examples:
  ✓ The Hillbilly Family
  ✓ The Cannibal Family
  ✓ The Professional Wrestling Family
  ✓ The Cheerleader Family (Figure A)
  ✓ The Pirate Family
  ✓ The Caveman Family
  ✓ The Underwater Family
  ✓ The Surfer Family (Figure B)
  ✓ The North Pole Nudist Family
  ✓ The Star Trek/Star Wars Family
  ✓ The Superhero Family
  ✓ The Gorilla Family
  ✓ The Space Alien Family
  ✓ The Halloween Family
  ✓ The Olympics Family

Leadership Tips:

- It may be easier for some groups to turn around instead of closing their eyes.
- After the group has played several rounds of using an assigned "family," invite the players to come up with their own ideas for families. Remind them that the goal is

for the other team to guess successfully, so they should choose a family everyone would know.
- If the group is especially large, you can divide them into more than two teams.
- To add variety, you can assign the same family to several groups to show at the same time or have one group create the photo while several groups guess.

Figure A. The Cheerleader Family

Figure B. The Surfer Family

#92: Initial Success

Objective: To think of as many famous people as possible with chosen initials
Recommended Ages: 10 and up
Number of Players: 4 to 40
Energy Level: 2 AMPS
Formation: Sitting in two teams

Description:

- Ask for a volunteer from each group who knows the American Sign Language alphabet to stand in the center, with their backs to the group. (This game doesn't require everyone to know the American Sign Language alphabet, but it's a must for the two volunteers).
- Tap one of the volunteers on the shoulder and then tell that person to silently perform the letters of the alphabet on his fingers. After about five seconds, signal the second volunteer to begin doing the same thing.
- After a few more seconds, tell both players to stop and face the group. Tell them to show the group the letter they were making when they were told to stop.
- Be sure that all the players know what the two letters are. Give both groups about a minute to make a list of as many famous people as they can with those initials.
- Then, alternate between the groups, asking them to name a famous person with those initials. For example, if the two letters were M and J, the groups could name Michael Jackson or Michael Jordan.,
- The group that gives more names without repeating one is the winner.

Leadership Tips:

- If the letters are an extra tough combination, announce before the groups begin that the order of the initials can be switched. For example, for M and J, the answers could include James Madison, John Mayer, and Joni Mitchell.
- If you play several rounds, have the volunteer signers start with the letter they finished with in the previous round.

#93: Lamina Sign Language

Objective: To guess the name of the animal that's being spelled backward
Recommended Ages: 10 and up
Number of Players: 3 to 30
Energy Level: 2 AMPS
Formation: Sitting in two or more teams

Description:

- Of the three American Sign Language games in this section, this is the only one that requires all players to know the American Sign Language alphabet.
- Have a volunteer stand in front of each team. Tell this person to begin slowly spelling the name of an animal with his hand. The trick is that the animal's name is being spelled backward.
- Explain that for a team to score, someone on that team must yell out the correct name of the animal before the word is completely spelled.

Leadership Tips:

- Longer words, such as "tnahpele" and "nekcihc," work best.
- To aid the speller, let him write out the name of the selected animal.

#94: Nine Birds

Objective: To solve a mental challenge
Recommended Ages: 10 and up
Number of Players: 10 to 100
Energy Level: 3 AMPS
Formation: Nine players sitting in three rows of three like a tic-tac-toe board, with enough room for someone to walk between them

Description:

- Prior to the beginning of the game, explain the rules to a volunteer player. Describe the three rows from left to right: Row #1 is the "this" row, Row #2 is the "that" row, and Row #3 is also a "this" row. Explain that if you refer to a bird in a "this" row and say "Is it *that* bird?" the answer is clearly yes. Whenever you use the word "this" on the "that" row or "that" on a "this" row, it's a signal that you're pointing to the selected bird. Using the correct word on the correct row simply means that person isn't the selected bird.

- To begin the game, tell the whole group that the nine players are all birds. Explain that when the volunteer turns his back someone will silently select one of the birds.
- Have the volunteer face the group. Ask him: "Is it this canary?"; "Is it that penguin?"; or "Is it that duck?"
- Tell the nine players to act like whatever bird you assign with your questions. The group will be amazed that the volunteer knows which bird was secretly selected. What kind of bird it is doesn't matter. What matters is that you and the volunteer understand the system. For example, if the middle person in the third row was secretly selected, point out that person to the assistant and say something such as "Is it that eagle?"

Leadership Tips:

- This is an extremely difficult challenge. Play some easier mind games first to warm up to this one.
- Give the group a hint by telling them to make each row the same kind of bird and then emphasize the "this" and the "that." Take it a step further by going sequentially down the rows. The ultimate hint: Point to a bird in a "this" row and say, "Is it *this* bird?" "No." Point to the same bird again and ask "Is it *that* bird?" "Yes!"
- To simplify this challenge, the leader can say "this" whenever it's not the selected bird and "that" whenever you point to the selected bird. Explain that the rows no longer matter. For example:

  Is it this bluebird?
  No.
  Is it this hawk?
  No.
  Is it this robin?
  No.
  Is it *that* falcon?
  Yes!

#95: One Hen

Objective: To follow the leader in a verbal chant
Recommended Ages: 10 and up
Number of Players: 1 and more
Energy Level: 1 AMPS
Formation: Sitting so all can hear the leader

Description:

- Memorize the following chant before you begin the game:
  One hen
  Two ducks
  Three squawking geese
  Four limerick oysters
  Five corpulent porpoises
  Six pairs of Revlon® tweezers
  Seven thousand Macedonians in full battle array
  Eight brass monkeys from the ancient sacred crypts of Egypt
  Nine apathetic, sympathetic, diabetic old men on roller skates with a marked propensity for procrastination and sloth
  Ten spherical, lyrical, diabolical denizens of the deep from the corners of the cove all at the same time … looking for love
- On the last line, feel free to be creative and personalize it for your group:
  ✓ … looking for fellowship and fun at Peace Presbyterian
  ✓ … looking for some tasty campers at Camp Makemie
- Tell the players to repeat what you say. As you say the chant, add one number each time for the group to repeat. For example:
  Leader: *One* hen
  Group: *One* hen
  Leader: *One* hen, *Two* ducks
  Group: *One* hen, *Two* ducks
  Leader: *One* hen, *Two* ducks, *Three* squawking geese … etc.

#96: One Noah's Ark

Objective: To follow the leader in a verbal chant
Recommended Ages: 8 and up
Number of Players: 2 to 100
Energy Level: 1 AMPS
Formation: Sitting so all can hear the leader

Description:

- Memorize the following chant before you begin the game:
  One Noah's Ark
  Two of every animal
  Three different types of sheep
  Four dozen different breeds of duck
  Five thousand buzzing members of the fly family
  Six empty cubits reserved for unicorns
  Seven uninvited termites
  Eight cranky, smelly, tired, seasick passengers shoveling quickly
  Nine 100 pound bags of super fresh, winter green, industrial-strength pet litter
  And lastly, *Ten* Commandments—let's remember 'em this time!
- Tell the players to repeat what you say. As you say the chant, add one number each time for the group to repeat. For example:
  Leader: *One* Noah's Ark
  Group: *One* Noah's Ark
  Leader: *One* Noah's Ark, *Two* of every animal
  Group: *One* Noah's Ark, *Two* of every animal
  Leader: *One* Noah's Ark, *Two* of every animal, *Three* different … etc.

Leadership Tip:

- This particular game works best with church groups, whereas #95: One Hen can be used with almost any group.

#97: See a Psychiatrist

Objective: To "diagnose" the group's problem
Recommended Ages: 10 and up
Number of Players: 8 or more
Energy Level: 2 AMPS
Formation: Sitting in a circle

Description:

- Ask a volunteer to leave the room. (It's best to select someone who enjoys a good challenge.) Explain that when he comes back he'll be the psychiatrist and will try to diagnose the group's problem.
- Tell the group that in this game the shared problem is that everyone in the circle believes he's the person on his *right*. If the group has just met recently, encourage the players to take a few minutes to get to know the people on the right and left.
- When the volunteer returns, tell him he can ask different individuals questions in order to figure out the group's problem.
- If the volunteer psychiatrist is getting too close to the correct diagnosis too quickly, the person answering may say, "I don't know. I think I need to see a psychiatrist." This is the cue for everyone in the circle to suddenly become the person on their *left*.

Leadership Tips:

- As the leader, you should drop hints to keep things moving and help the volunteer when necessary by suggesting questions such as "Ask someone what they're wearing."
- It's okay for the volunteer to be a little embarrassed at first, but be sure that this person is never made to look foolish or stupid.
- Help the volunteer by requesting that the group limit the "I don't know" response to twice in the round. If the volunteer is stumped, the group can help by giving very precise answers about what they're wearing or that they "aren't feeling like themselves."

#98: Belly Laugh

Objective: To see how long the group can go without laughing
Recommended Ages: 6 and up
Number of Players: 6 or more
Energy Level: 2 AMPS
Formation: Standing

Description:

- Have the players lie on the floor one at a time so each person is resting his head on the stomach of the player before him, creating a zigzag pattern.
- Tell the players not to laugh or giggle.
- Tell the first person to say "Ha," the second person to say "Ha, ha," the third one to say "Ha, ha, ha," and so on, down the line until someone actually laughs.
- Because the real goal of the game is lots of laughter, once someone laughs, the group can either start over where they left off and see if they can go longer without laughing or just keep going until everyone laughs.

Leadership Tips:

- This activity can also be used as a drama exercise to assist people in not laughing and breaking character.
- Know your group. Because touch is involved, risk is involved. If even one person would be uncomfortable playing this game, don't play it! Choose a different activity.

#99: Story Jumble

Objective: To figure out who's telling the selected story
Recommended Ages: 10 and up
Number of Players: 6 to 30
Energy Level: 3 AMPS
Formation: Standing in teams of 15 or less

Description:

- Set up the teams and then ask each team to secretly select a storyteller.
- Announce the title of a well-known bedtime story, such as "Goldilocks and the Three Bears" "The Three Little Pigs," "Cinderella," etc. Tell the storyteller to think about the selected story and then tell the others on the team to think about any other story in the entire world.
- Choose one team to go first. Tell the players that when you give the signal to begin that everyone on the starting team should begin telling his story by silently mouthing for 15 seconds. Encourage all players to be as animated and enthusiastic as possible.
- When time is up, point to each member of the telling team and then ask the players in the other groups to vote on who they think was the person telling the story you originally announced.
- Repeat the game for the other teams.
- If you play a second round, have everyone on a team tell the story out loud at the same time.
- In the third round, tell the players to be silent once more but to pantomime their stories as actively as possible.

Leadership Tips:

- When all three rounds are over, ask players which round they found most difficult and why.
- You can lead a discussion about what happens when people all try talking at the same time or what happens when someone tries to communicate while others are causing distractions or aren't listening.

#100: Who's Knocking at My Door?

Objective: To guess who's knocking
Recommended Ages: 6 and up
Number of Players: 6 or more
Energy Level: 2 AMPS
Formation: Sitting in a circle

Description:

- Have a first volunteer stand in the middle of the circle and put on a blindfold.
- Ask the group to secretly choose a second volunteer, who will stand and face the first volunteer. Tell the second volunteer to make a pretend "knocking" noise with his mouth.
- Have the first volunteer say "Who's that knocking at my door?" and the second volunteer respond with "One of Santa's elves, collecting for the poor."
- Explain that it's the goal of the blindfolded person to guess who the second volunteer is. The goal of the second volunteer to disguise his voice as much as possible to fool the first person.
- If the first volunteer successfully guesses the identity of the second volunteer, the second volunteer becomes the new blind guesser. If the first volunteer is unsuccessful, send a new volunteer to knock.
- This game will lead to a lot of silly voices and lots of laughs.

Leadership Tips:

- This game works best with groups that have had time to get to know each other first.
- Feel free to replace "Santa's elves" with a do-gooder suitable to your group.

#101: Hugs and Shrugs

Objective: To affirm other people in the group
Recommended Ages: 10 and up
Number of Players: 6 to 100
Energy Level: 3 AMPS
Formation: Standing in pairs, with partners facing each other

Description:

- Explain that one of the partners will shout "Hugs or shrugs!"
- Tell each of the partners to show each other one or two fingers. If the sum total of the fingers is even, the players are to give each other a compliment. If the sum total of fingers is odd, the players are to give each other a hug or another sign of affirmation.
- Instruct the players to find a new partner and then continue the game.

Leadership Tips:

- This is a good closing activity for a group that has bonded and played well together.
- The hug can be changed to a high five, fist bump, or another affirming gesture if hugs aren't appropriate for the group.

Appendix A
Creating Your Own Programs

While the games in this book are ideal for spontaneous fun or filling time creatively and constructively with a group, you can also put the games together for hours of ice-breaking and group-building recreation. Fellowship suppers, family reunions, and youth retreats are great settings for this kind of structured fun.

Creating a program that keeps participants interested and engaged is an art that's not difficult to learn, especially if you keep in mind the following three basic principles:

- *Know where and how your group is beginning.* Will they be arriving individually, as if coming to a meeting or party? Will they have already been together as a group in a single location, such as a retreat?
- *Know what you want to accomplish with the group.* Are they meeting for the first time and need to get to know each other? Are they young adults who have been sitting a long time and need to expend energy constructively? Are they a group that needs to learn how to work together to solve a problem?
- *Know how you want the group to end up when you've finished with the program.* Will they need to become quiet and attentive for a study time? Do they need to get fired up to do some hard work?

Using the chart in Appendix B, you can select games that meet your needs in terms of age, group size, energy level, and formation. Planning ahead is important. It's easy to kill momentum by changing formation or energy level without apparent reason. For example, imagine moving from a quiet circle game to a high-energy tag game to quieting down to learn rules to a more complicated game and then get back in a circle. Dramatic shifts can cause the group to lose its focus.

Instead, a program that is well planned and takes the needs of the group into consideration builds its own momentum. Imagine a group mingling in a mixer game, then moving to partners, then to some high-energy circle games, then a few games with lower energy, and finally quieting down with a mind game. A well-led recreation program is like an orchestra building to a crescendo, leaving the participants feeling good about what they've just done.

Four example programs follow. Each is designed to last about one hour and focus on a different type of group. You can use these just as they are or adapt them to fit your needs. To help you understand the reasons these programs work, the lists are annotated to show the "flow," so you can see how the momentum builds.

Program Example #1: Youth

Number of Players: 20 to 30
Setting: Flat grassy field or gym/fellowship hall

- #5: Here I Sit in the Grass (circle—mixer)
- #4: Get to Know You Marathon (line—mixer)
- #8: Partner Mixer (mixer)
- #14: Fast Math (group game)
- #90: Walking Tag (energy game)
- #88: Spinning Wool (energy game)
- #83: Barnyard Hens (energy game)
- #42: Gotcha (circle game)
- #82: Wolf in Sheep's Clothing (energy game)
- #11: Aardvarks, Ducks, and Lambs (group game)
- #86: I'm Late, I'm Late, I'm Late … (energy game)
- #31: About-Face (circle game)
- #48: Wanna Buy a Duck? (circle game)

Program Example #2: Young Elementary

Number of Players: 20 to 30
Setting: Outdoor flat area or indoor gym-style area

- #7: Name Zoom (mixer)
- #29: Touch Twister (mixer)
- #14: Fast Math (group)
- #85: Hook 'Em (circle)
- #33: Are You the Spy? (circle)
- #31: About-Face (circle)
- #44: Noah's Ark (circle)
- #42: Gotcha (circle)
- #38: Considering Cap (circle)
- #24: Simon Says Time Warp (group)
- #84: Everyone's "It" Tag (group)
- #27: Statues (group)

If time allows:
- #55: Costume Party (mind)
- #57: Fantastic Fruits (Big Fruits/Little Fruits) (mind)
- #95: One Hen (silly)

Program Example #3: Intergenerational

Number of Players: 25 to 50
Setting: Outdoors or a social hall

- #75: Imagination Toss (group builder)
- #8: Partner Mixer (mixer)
- #28: Thumb Grab (group)
- #41: Eye Contact (circle)
- #32: Anatomy Lesson (circle)
- #46: Spontaneous Zoo (circle)
- #49: What's Your Sign? (circle)
- #45: One Frog (circle)
- #47: This Is an Eagle (circle)
- #21: Machine Charades (group)
- #9: Name-Dropper (group)
- #16: Firecrackers (group)

If time allows:
- #61: Twin Cities (mind)
- #96: One Noah's Ark (silly)
- #100: Who's Knocking at My Door? (silly)

Program Example #4: Older Adults

Number of Players: 10 to 50
Setting: Social hall or picnic shelter

- #2: Amazing Adjective (mixer)
- #1: 15-Second Autobiography (mixer)
- #15: Sign Language Shoot-Out (silly)
- #13: Echoes and Double Echoes (group)
- #99: Story Jumble (silly)
- #36: Catch the Leader (circle)
- #50: Zip-Zap-Pop (circle)
- #37: Categories (circle)
- #39: Countdown (circle)
- #23: Rain Dance (group)
- #52: Bang-Bang-Bang (mind)
- #101: Hugs and Shrugs (group)

Appendix B
Games Chart

Game Number	Game Name	AMPS	Formation	Minimum Number of People	Maximum Number of People	Minimum Age	Category	Name Game
1	15-Second Autobiography	2	Partners	4	100	12	Mixer	X
2	Amazing Adjective	1	Circle	5	30	8	Mixer	X
3	Cliché Mixer Party Starter	2	Other	6	30	10	Mixer	
4	Get to Know You Marathon	6	Boundaries	2	50	6	Mixer	
5	Here I Sit in the Grass	6	Circle	8	50	5	Mixer	X
6	King Nebuchadnezzar	3	Circle	6	30	8	Mixer	X
7	Name Zoom	2	Circle	8	30	8	Mixer	X
8	Partner Mixer	4	Partners	10	100	6	Mixer	X
9	Name-Dropper	5	Teams	10	50	8	Mixer	X
10	Sound Effect Name Game	1	Circle	4	20	7	Mixer	X
11	Aardvarks, Ducks, and Lambs	9	Circle	12	60	6	Group	
12	Cliché Shout	2	Lines	12	20	10	Group	
13	Echoes and Double Echoes	2	Partners	2	100	10	Group	
14	Fast Math	2	Partners	2	100	8	Group	
15	Sign Language Shoot-Out	3	Partners	2	200	7	Group	
16	Firecrackers	4	Wide open	10	40	8	Group	
17	Gossip/ Physical Gossip	2	Lines	5	50	8	Group	
18	Without Anyone Else Knowing …	3	Wide open	6	100	10	Group	
19	Human Keyboard	4	Circle	20	100	10	Group	

Game Number	Game Name	AMPS	Formation	Minimum Number of People	Maximum Number of People	Minimum Age	Category	Name Game
20	Spy	4	Wide open	10	50	8	Group	
21	Machine Charades	5	Teams	8	100	6	Group	
22	North and South	8	Partners	9	100	10	Group	
23	Rain Dance	3	Wide open	5	100	5	Group	
24	Simon Says Time Warp	6	Wide open	10	100	7	Group	
25	Simon Says Swap	6	Teams	10	100	8	Group	
26	Singing Charades	3	Teams	6	50	None	Group	
27	Statues	3	Other	7	30	8	Group	
28	Thumb Grab	3	Partners	2	100	None	Group	
29	Touch Twister	4	Other	8	50	6	Group	
30	Two-Team Spelling Bee	3	Teams	9	30	10	Group	
31	About-Face	8	Circle	20	100	8	Circle	
32	Anatomy Lesson	3	Circle	4	30	4	Circle	
33	Are You the Spy?	8	Circle	12	50	8	Circle	
34	Big Bunny	6	Circle	10	50	8	Circle	
35	C'mon	10	Circle	12	30	18	Circle	
36	Catch the Leader	6	Circle	5	20	5	Circle	
37	Categories	2	Circle	4	30	6	Circle	
38	Considering Cap	5	Circle	6	30	6	Circle	
39	Countdown	2	Circle	8	25	8	Circle	
40	Cross Your Palms	5	Circle	5	20	5	Circle	
41	Eye Contact	5	Circle	8	30	8	Circle	
42	Gotcha	7	Circle	5	30	6	Circle	
43	Just Like	1	Circle	5	50	7	Circle	X

Game Number	Game Name	AMPS	Formation	Minimum Number of People	Maximum Number of People	Minimum Age	Category	Name Game
44	Noah's Ark	5	Circle	6	30	6	Circle	
45	One Frog	2	Circle	5	15	8	Circle	
46	Spontaneous Zoo	6	Circle	6	50	None	Circle	
47	This Is an Eagle	2	Circle	5	30	5	Circle	
48	Wanna Buy a Duck?	2	Circle	5	30	6	Circle	
49	What's Your Sign?	5	Circle	6	30	7	Circle	
50	Zip-Zap-Pop	3	Circle	6	30	None	Circle	
51	Zoom and Mooz	3	Circle	5	50	None	Circle	
52	Bang-Bang-Bang	1	Sitting (not circle)	3	30	8	Mind	
53	Bugs	1	Sitting (not circle)	3	50	8	Mind	
54	Cash Only Store	2	Sitting (not circle)	2	50	8	Mind	
55	Costume Party	1	Sitting (not circle)	3	30	8	Mind	
56	Draw the Man	2	Sitting (not circle)	3	30	6	Mind	
57	Fantastic Fruits (Big Fruits/Little Fruits)	1	Sitting (not circle)	4	50	8	Mind	
58	I Like Apples	1	Sitting (not circle)	3	50	8	Mind	
59	Number Magic	1	Sitting (not circle)	3	50	8	Mind	
60	Picnic	1	Sitting (not circle)	3	30	8	Mind	
61	Twin Cities	1	Sitting (not circle)	3	50	10	Mind	
62	Adverb	4	Sitting (not circle)	6	50	10	Drama	
63	B-Movie Voice-Over Theater	5	Lines	10	50	10	Drama	
64	Emotion Relay	9	Other	12	60	10	Drama	
65	Freeze	6	Circle	6	20	10	Drama	
66	Hitchhiker	6	Lines	8	50	10	Drama	

Game Number	Game Name	AMPS	Formation	Minimum Number of People	Maximum Number of People	Minimum Age	Category	Name Game
67	Please/No	3	Circle	4	30	6	Drama	
68	Smile Gauntlet	4	Lines	10	40	10	Drama	
69	Train Station/ Bus Stop	5	Lines	6	30	10	Drama	
70	Whopper	2	Sitting (not circle)	2	30	10	Drama	
71	Wipe That Smile Off Your Face	3	Circle	6	50	10	Drama	
72	Clap On, Clap Off!	6	Sitting (not circle)	5	50	10	Group Builder	
73	Freeway Follies	7	Partners	8	30	12	Group Builder	
74	Hike in the Dark	5	Partners	4	30	12	Group Builder	
75	Imagination Toss	6	Circle	8	20	10	Group Builder	X
76	Photographer	3	Partners	8	30	10	Group Builder	
77	Suey, Suey	5	Partners	4	30	12	Group Builder	
78	Timeline	3	Lines	8	30	10	Group Builder	
79	Spot	6	Partners	4	30	12	Group Builder	
80	Go With the Flow	6	Circle	9	36	12	Group Builder	
81	Parting of the Sea	6	Lines	4	30	12	Group Builder	
82	Wolf in Sheep's Clothing	10	Teams	20	60	10	Energy	
83	Barnyard Hens	9	Wide open	20	200	8	Energy	
84	Everyone's "It" Tag	9	Boundaries	10	100	8	Energy	
85	Hook 'Em	9	Partners	7	100	8	Energy	
86	I'm Late, I'm Late, I'm Late …	8	Circle	12	60	7	Energy	
87	Partners Tag	9	Partners	2	100	6	Energy	
88	Spinning Wool	9	Other	4	100	8	Energy	
89	Tentacle Tag	8	Boundaries	10	100	6	Energy	
90	Walking Tag	8	Partners	10	100	8	Energy	

Game Number	Game Name	AMPS	Formation	Minimum Number of People	Maximum Number of People	Minimum Age	Category	Name Game
91	Family Photo	3	Teams	6	30	12	Silly	
92	Initial Success	2	Other	4	40	10	Silly	
93	Lamina Sign Language	2	Sitting (not circle)	3	30	10	Silly	
94	Nine Birds	3	Other	10	100	10	Silly	
95	One Hen	1	Sitting (not circle)	1	50	10	Silly	
96	One Noah's Ark	1	Sitting (not circle)	2	100	8	Silly	
97	See a Psychiatrist	2	Circle	8	30	10	Silly	
98	Belly Laugh	2	Other	6	20	6	Silly	
99	Story Jumble	3	Teams	6	30	10	Silly	
100	Who's Knocking at My Door?	2	Sitting (not circle)	6	30	6	Silly	
101	Hugs and Shrugs	3	Partners	6	100	10	Silly	

Appendix C
American Sign Language Alphabet

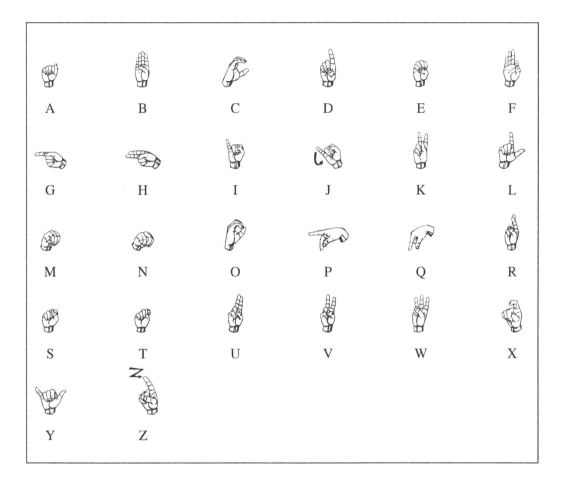

The American Sign Language letters were created using the Gallaudet font from Insect Bytes. The Gallaudet font is copyright © 1991 by David Rakowski. All rights reserved. Used with permission.

Resources for Recreation Leaders

Books

50 Ways to Use Your Noodle: Loads of Land Games with Foam Noodle Toys by Sam Sikes and Chris Cavert (Learning Unlimited, 1997). This book includes numerous activities for fun and group building.

101 Age-Appropriate Camp Activities by Jared R. Knight (Healthy Learning, 2008). This book solves one of the major recreation challenges—designing and creating social recreation programs that are appropriate for each age group.

101 Games & Gimmicks for Kid People by Steven Peck (Healthy Learning, 2010). This book provides a wide variety of games and activities that can be used with people of all ages. Also check out Peck's other recreation resources (also available from Healthy Learning).

Grab-and-Go Activities: Games to Play With Kids in God's World and *Grab-and-Go Activities: More Games to Play With Kids in God's World* by Faith Evans (Healthy Learning, 2010). These books are designed to go into counselor backpacks as a quick resource for activities.

Guide for Recreation Leaders by Glenn Bannerman and Bob Fakkema (Bridge Resources; revised edition, 1998). If you want to be a better recreation leader who invites participation from all ages, this book is worth your time.

Non-Competitive Games for People of All Ages by Susan Butler (Bethany House, 1986). This book includes a good variety of games and is easy to use.

Quicksilver: Adventure Games, Initiative Problems, Trust Activities and a Guide to Effective Leadership by Karl Rohnke and Steve Butler (Kendall/Hunt Publishing, 1995). This book was written by one of the definitive leaders in the world of teambuilding activities and technique. Also check out Rohnke's other resources that reflect his decades of experience working with Project Adventure.

Recreation Express by Lee Cross and Beth Gunn. An interactive database with over 100 games that helps the user create recreation programs like those in Chapter 11 based on age groups, energy level, etc.—great for those who want to keep track of programs they create. Available at www.recreationexpress.com.

Workshops

Annual Recreation Workshop (www.recreationworkshop.org) in Montreat, North Carolina, is held annually the first full week in May. Excellent leaders teach basic and advanced recreation leadership in a variety of areas.

Project Adventure (www.pa.org) is the world leader in training teambuilding and challenge course facilitators.

Southern Annual Recreation Workshop (www.sarw.net) is a weekend whirlwind of learning with many of the same instructors as the Annual Recreation Workshop.

About the Authors

Anthony Burcher is the summer assistant director at Makemie Woods Camp and Conference Center. During the school year, he is an outreach teacher for the Jamestown-Yorktown Foundation, helping kids learn history hands-on with artifacts and experiential learning. His favorite job is as a professional storyteller, as he recounts with much humor growing up in the rural South. Sample stories can be found at www.anthonyburcher.com.

The Rev. **Michelle "Mike" Burcher** is the director of the Makemie Woods Camp and Conference Center. An ordained Presbyterian minister, she has also served as a small church pastor and as a campus minister, and has taught at the Presbyterian School of Christian Education. Her favorite hobby is exploring caves.

Together, the Burchers have over 50 years of camp and recreation leadership experience. They have taught numerous workshops about leadership, storytelling, sharing faith stories, and working with children with ADHD, and are constantly adding to their repertoire of "no prop" activities. They have two grown children and a menagerie of critters.